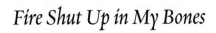

Fire Shut Up in My Bones

Fire Shut Up in My Bones

A Memoir

CHARLES M. BLOW

HOUGHTON MIFFLIN HARCOURT
Boston   New York
2014

For information about permission to reproduce selections from this book,
write to Permissions, Houghton Mifflin Harcourt Publishing Company,
215 Park Avenue South, New York, New York 10003.

www.hmhco.com

Library of Congress Cataloging-in-Publication Data
Blow, Charles M., date.
Fire shut up in my bones : a memoir / Charles M. Blow.
pages cm
ISBN 978-0-544-22804-7 (hardcover)
1. Blow, Charles M., date. 2. Journalists — United States — Biography.
3. African American journalists — Biography. I. Title.
PN4874.B575A3 2014
070.92—dc23
[B]   2014006729

Book design by Greta Sibley

Printed in the United States of America
DOC 10 9 8 7 6 5 4 3 2 1

Author's Note: Nearly all names of people in this book have been changed.
No place names or other details have been altered. Some passages in this
book were previously published in the *New York Times*.

To my mother, who is my rock.
To my children, who are my reasons.

CONTENTS

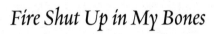

Fire Shut Up in My Bones

PROLOGUE

Tears flowed out of me from a walled-off place, from another time, from a little boy who couldn't cry.

I had held on to the hurt and shame and doubt for so long, balling it up in the pit of me, that I never thought it would come out, or that it could. I certainly didn't think it would come out like this. Not in a flash. But there it was.

Some of my tears streamed over the arc of my cheeks and off the rim of my jaw. Others rounded the corners of my nose and puddled in the crease of my lips. I didn't wipe them. I wore them.

I looked over at the rusting pistol on the passenger seat. It was a .22 with a long black barrel and a wooden grip. It was the gun my mother had insisted I take with me to college, "just in case." I had grabbed it from beneath my seat when I jumped into the car. I cast glances at it as I drove. I had to convince myself that I was indeed about to use it.

The ridges of the gas pedal pressed into the flesh of my foot as I raced down Interstate 20 toward my mother's house, just twenty-five miles away. I had driven this lonely stretch of north Louisiana road from college to home a hundred times. It had never gone so slowly; I had never driven so fast.

I began to scream as a fresh round of tears erupted. "Mother-fucker!" I slammed my fists down on the steering wheel over and over. "No! No! . . . Ah! Ah!" In part I was letting it out. In part I was pumping myself up. I had never thought myself capable of killing. I was a twenty-year-old college student. But I was about to kill a man. My own cousin. Chester.

Minutes earlier I was in my apartment at school doing much of nothing, just pushing back against sorrow as it pressed down. My mother called. She told me someone wanted to speak to me. There was a silence on the line, and then words: "What's going on, boy?"

It was Chester. He was at my mother's house, at our house. It had been years since I had heard that voice. "What's going on, boy?" like nothing had ever happened, like everything was buried and forgotten. But betrayal doesn't work that way. Even when it's buried, it doesn't stay buried. It's still alive, down there, scratching its way back to the surface. It must be buried over and over again.

I don't recall saying anything or even hanging up. I flung myself down the stairs of the apartment wearing only pajama pants and a T-shirt. No shoes. I burst out of the door and bolted to the car.

I was fully engulfed in an irrepressible rage. Everything in me was churning and pumping and boiling. All reason and restraint were lost to it. I was about to do something I wouldn't be able to undo. Bullets and blood and death. I gave myself over to the idea.

The scene from the night when I was seven years old kept replaying in my mind: me waking up to him pushed up behind me, his arms locked around me, my underwear down around my thighs. The weight of the guilt and grieving that followed. The years of his bullying designed to keep me from telling, and the years of questioning my role in his betrayal.

It was that betrayal, I believed, that had first caused a curiosity about guys to bleed into my attraction to girls. My lost innocence had to be avenged. My conflict had to be quelled. That is why he had to die. That is why I had to kill him.

I was convinced that if I removed him from the world, the part of me that I despised would go with him. A second wrong would restore me to right.

I

The House with No Steps

The first memory I have in the world is of death and tears. That is how I would mark the beginning of my life: the way people mark the end of one.

My family had gathered at Papa Joe's house because Mam' Grace was slipping away, only I didn't register it that way. For some reason I thought that it was her birthday.

Papa Joe was my great-grandfather. Mam' Grace was his laid-up wife who passed the days in a hospital bed squeezed into their former den, looking out through a large picture window that faced the street, watching the world she was leaving literally pass her by.

We were in the living room when he called to us.

"I thank she 'bout to go." I didn't know what that meant. I thought it was time to give her a gift.

With that, my family filed into her room, surrounding her with love. Their hearts were heavy. Mine, though, was light. I thought we were about to give her something special. They knew something special was about to be taken away.

She peacefully drew her last breath as her head tilted, and she fell still.

No dramatic death rattle, no fear-tinged soliloquy, no last-minute confession. Like a raft pushed gently from the shore, she drifted quietly from now into forever — a beautiful life, beautifully surrendered.

But I recorded it differently. I thought she turned to see a gift that wasn't there, and that something went tragically wrong in the turning.

When Mam' Grace left the room she took the air with her. No one could breathe. They could only scream.

My mother was overcome. She ran from the house, and I ran behind her. She threw herself to the ground near the hog pen, wailing, her back rocking against it. I shooed the hogs away as they tried to lap at her hair. I was too young to know what it meant to die, but tears I knew. Sorrow flooded out of my mother like a dam had broken. It was one, though, that she would soon rebuild, taller and stronger than it had been. As a child, I would never see her cry again.

I spent most of my life believing my three-year-old's version of what happened that day, until as an adult I recounted my memory to my mother and she set the story straight — our gathering at Mam' Grace's bedside was not to celebrate the day she was born but to accept that it was her day to die.

My mother's telling of it seemed more fitting. As a child I became accustomed to death spectacles. I went to more funerals than birthday parties. My mother took me even when she left my older brothers behind. She thought me too young to stay home with them. I was also too young to understand what I was seeing at the funerals. My brothers once asked me how the dead man had looked at one of the services. I responded as a child would: "Good, I guess. He was jus' up there sleepin' in a big ol' suitcase."

. . .

I was born in the summer of 1970, the last of five boys stretched over eight years. My parents were a struggling young couple who had been married one afternoon under a shade tree by a preacher without a church. No guests or fancy dress, just the two of them, lost in love, and the preacher taking a break from working on a house.

By the time I came along, my mother was a dutiful wife growing dead-ass tired of working on a dead-end marriage and a dead-end job. My father was a construction worker by trade, a pool shark by habit, and a serial philanderer by compulsion.

My mother was a stout woman with a man's name — Billie. She was plain-faced with honest eyes — no black grease by the lash line, no blue powder on the lids, eyebrows not plucked up high and thin. She used only a stroke of lipstick, dark like a fig, and a little powder to cover the acne that still popped up under the balls of the cheeks that sat high on her face.

My father was short for a man, with a child's plaything for a name — Spinner. He had flawless dark brown skin and a head full of big, wet-looking curls, black as oil. And he had the smile of a scoundrel — the kind of smile that disarmed men and undressed women.

We lived in the rural north Louisiana town of Gibsland, nearly halfway between Shreveport and Monroe and right in the middle of nowhere. The town was named after a slave owner named Gibbs whose plantation it had been. Its only claim to fame was that Bonnie and Clyde had been killed just south of town in 1934. Townspeople still relished the infamy. Gibsland was a place where the line between heroes and villains was not so clearly drawn.

Although the town was already contracting, downtown retained a one-of-each-thing, much-of-nothing quaintness. There was one grocery store and one dry cleaner. One feed-and-seed and one drugstore. One dry goods store and one bank. One restaurant and one furniture store. One stoplight and one policeman.

It was a place with whites and blacks mostly separated by a shallow ditch and a deep understanding. Main Street cut through town from north to south and was flanked on both sides by most of the white community. Most blacks, like my family, lived on the western side of town.

Ours was a small, rent-to-own house on a narrow street — Third Street — that ran down a gently sloping hill. The street was populated with young families and old couples — everybody nickname-close. I wasn't only the youngest boy in my family, I was the youngest boy in the whole neighborhood — not just my mother's baby, but everybody's baby, a fact expressed in a nickname of my own: Char'esBaby. That was what everyone but the single mother next door, a round woman with three round sons, called me. She insisted on Chocolate. She said that my skin looked "just like chocolate." Every time she saw me, she met me with a smile and a request: "Come here and give me some sugar, Chocolate."

Our house had a small, uneven yard dotted with fire ant mounds, prickly weeds, and clover patches, but little grass. It had an unpaved driveway and a three-foot-high front porch with no steps. This meant that you had to either jump up onto the porch or, as was more often the case, enter through the back. My mother pleaded with my father to build steps. He could easily have done it, construction being his trade and all, but he never did.

A lone pink-flowered mimosa tree stood near the street, stunted and distorted, bowing to passersby and drawing a charm of humming-birds. A large sweetgum tree marked the property line, its muscular, runoff-exposed roots cascading into a ditch — twisting terrain for secondhand action figures and a handful of Hot Wheels. Wasp nests dangled from the overhangs. Paint strips peeled away from the house like husks from corn. Son of a Bitch, a dog my brothers found — they begged my mother to let them give it its literal name — sought refuge in cool spots under the house.

I don't remember much about my brothers in that house, only that I shared a room with my oldest brother, Nathan, and that my next-to-oldest and next-to-youngest brothers, William and Robert, shared the adjoining room.

Theirs was the only bedroom in the house with a television, up on a chest of drawers between twin beds. That meant that their room served as a den by default. We had pillow fights and tickle fights in that room. We draped sheets over box fans to make inflated tents. We watched *Soul Train,* lighting up at the dancers getting down, joining in as they ended the show: "Love, peace, and soooouuul!" There was a hole in the wall that joined our closets, just big enough for me to squeeze through and make repeated "surprise!" entries into William and Robert's room. To do so, I had to crawl over a bunch of old guitars that littered the closet floors like limbs blown down by a heavy storm.

Nathan told me that they belonged to my father, that he had been in a band, that one night after a gig and a little too much liquor my father and his bandmates had a car wreck. My father was driving. Someone in the band was killed in the crash. My father did a stint in prison for his part in it. When he got out, he never played again. That's when he took up construction.

After my parents married, my mother was pregnant every couple of years, and perpetually recovering from or falling victim to illness. She was so sick when I was born that my maternal grandmother, whom we called Big Mama, took me to live with her and her fourth husband, Jed, in Arkansas, until my mother got better. Big Mama had also taken in my middle brother, James, before me. I stayed with them in Arkansas for three years before coming home. James never came home.

So, two or three times a month, my parents, my brothers, and I piled into our battered Volkswagen Beetle for the hourlong drive to visit them. Everyone else found a seat. I curled up in the package tray under the back window, the engine buzzing beneath me as I stared up at silent congregations of clouds floating across the skies.

On the way to the interstate we passed what folks called Boogie Woogie Road, the first road past the city limits on the west side of town. My mother told us that the road was named for the white man black folks called Boogie Woogie, who had run the now-abandoned, dirt-floor store at the junction where the road met the highway. But there were other reasons for the name that my mother refused to relay. Boogie Woogie was a long, straight road that descended a hill with several drops and as many plateaus, but only a few houses. It was perfect for racing hot rods by day and parking with a sweetheart by night. Boogie Woogie.

Just past Boogie Woogie Road was Martin's Pond. It was the pond my mother insisted was bottomless, because she had always been told it was, even though the stump of a cypress tree rose from the center of it. "Mama, it cain't be bottomless," we'd say, giggling. "Yes it is," she'd insist, only half jokingly.

When we reached Interstate 20 we took it for as long as we could. The road cut a path over rolling hills, which in spots were blanketed by stands of farmed pines, spaced like soldiers — in perfect rows, same age, same height. In other spots, virgin forest was being consumed by kudzu, a big-leafed, invasive weed from East Asia enveloping whole swaths of the American South, growing so fast that folks called it the mile-a-minute vine, blanketing acres of shrubs and trees.

When we turned off the interstate, we took winding roads through small towns with sweet names like Dixie Inn and Plain Dealing; through stretches devoid of people, save an occasional farmhouse set far back from the road or a country café like the one called Ho-Made; and through vast landscapes of cotton fields — endless rows of brown plants stippled by hypnotic flecks of white.

My mother told us stories of the black folk who used to work the fields before machines pushed them out, the pickers dragging long, teardrop-shaped bags they filled with one hundred pounds of featherweight cotton fibers plucked from unforgiving bolls that shredded the fingers by day's end.

She seemed to relish telling such stories — their power to educate and evoke, to turn our minds, to divert them from our own harsh realities.

We rarely stopped along the way, but if we did, it was for gas, or a Coke, or a rummage sale, which my mother scoured compulsively.

Occasionally we burst into song when a favorite tune came on the radio.

> Bad, bad, Leroy Brown
> The baddest man in the whole damn town . . .

These were good times, family times — all crammed together in that tiny car, with no choice but to talk and sing and bind ourselves to one another.

Soon we were pulling into Big Mama and Jed's yard, while they stood on the porch to greet us, smiling and waving.

Their Arkansas community was even smaller than Gibsland. For reasons unknown, it was called Kiblah, a name derived from the Arabic *Kaaba,* the cube structure at the center of the mosque in Mecca, the holiest place, the House of God.

Kiblah was that for me, my place apart from the traumas of struggle and the need of things. There my spirit floated, without weight or worry, like a leaf upon a still water. It was home, in a way, my first home, and Jed, Big Mama, and James were my first family. It was there that I learned the meaning of love from Jed, the man I counted as my first father, although he was neither my father nor blood family.

The house itself was tiny, with five rooms. It was set on a small patch of land perilously close to Highway 71 and between a forest on one side and the expansive cow pasture of a white farmer on the other. My brothers and I played in the dusty front yard. Traffic whizzed by just a few feet away from our ball games and bike riding.

There was no gas heat or running water and no bathroom. For washing, cooking, and drinking, we drew water from the well in the front yard, and heated it on the wood-burning stove. Clothes were hand-washed in a number 2 washtub on the back porch. We bathed out there in that same washtub, sometimes in the laundry water.

Big Mama was a big woman with a big laugh. Everything about her seemed to be outsized — big hips, big bosom, big heart, big voice.

Everything big. But she was aging. Her top molars were missing and her short hair was thinning.

Jed was a chain smoker with a strong back and soft eyes. It was those eyes that struck you — brown, maple-syrup sweet, a hint of gray around the edges, sunrise yellow where the whites should be; deep enough to get lost in, bottomless like Martin's Pond; damp like the beginning of a good cry or the end of a good laugh. They were the kind of eyes that saw down into the dark of you and drew up the light; the kind that melted worry like a stick of butter near a warm stove; the kind that forgave secret shame before it scarred the throat on the way out.

It would take a man with eyes like that to make Big Mama move to the middle of nowhere and bathe outside.

In fact, this was my grandmother's second stint in Arkansas. She had moved there once before, to marry another man after she and my grandfather, her first husband, broke up. My mother didn't follow. She stayed behind in Louisiana with Mam' Grace. But soon the man died and Big Mama was back in Louisiana, living with my mother and my great-uncle Paul at Mam' Grace and Papa Joe's house.

Then she married for a third time. Again, it didn't last long. He left her one day after realizing that she'd been spending the car-note money on clothes and shoes. He only became aware of the deceit when a man came to repossess the car. He was outraged. There must be some misunderstanding, he said to the man; his wife had paid the bill every month, on time. He had the receipts to prove it. Unfortunately, he could only find one — an old one.

Big Mama had been giving her husband the same receipt every month, claiming it was evidence of a new payment and stealing it back from him when he put it away. He was illiterate, and he trusted her. Now he was furious, and done. He grabbed two bags of stuff he had been storing in the smokehouse, "rats and all" was the family joke, and that was the end.

But that woman existed a world away from the grandmother I knew, the one now married to Jed.

The only remnant of Big Mama's past was a water-damaged, hand-tinted portrait of her and a man I didn't recognize, both sugar-sharp, sitting on a bench in front of a painted backdrop. He was sitting up tall and strong. She was laughing, legs crossed, her head resting delicately on his shoulder. There was a power in his pose, but there was more in hers, a feminine power, the kind that lights a room and buckles a knee, the kind that makes men do things they know they shouldn't—sneak in through open windows, lie to loved ones, give more than they have.

I often stared at that picture, trying to connect that woman—young, thin, radiant, dangerously alluring—with the woman I knew now as Big Mama. I couldn't do it.

She was different now. Jed had made her different because he was more powerful than she was. He drew his power from a different source—not from hollowness but from wholeness. It was a grand, simple kind of power. It came from the knowing and accepting and loving of self that made the knowing and accepting and loving of everything else possible. It didn't crush, but accommodated. He hadn't taken away Big Mama's power but given her a peaceful place to harness and transform it, to calm down and grow up, to move out of the woman she had been and into the woman she could be.

She was like a river—always running, never still, wanting to be somewhere other than where it was—that had finally reached the ocean—vast and deep and exactly where it was always meant to be.

He did the same for all of us—made us feel that we had finally made it to where we were always meant to be, the place where we could stop running and just relax. He made us all better than we had been, not so much by any one thing I remember him doing, but by the gentle, calming spirit that seemed to emanate from his being. That was the kind of father I wished I had.

And James was the brother I felt closest to, even though he lived far away. Maybe it was because we had been raised together, just the two of us, when I was a baby. Maybe it was because he too was now a bit of a loner, being raised as an only child in the middle of nowhere. Or maybe it was because I thought him the smartest of my brothers. Whatever it was, he seemed to me special and different.

He was lighter-skinned that the rest of us, the recipient of a recessive gene, I suppose, and he had his own room and more toys than us, new toys bought from a store, not come across at a rummage sale. And most of all he had Jed, all the time.

But in the summer of 1974 Jed built the house that he would die in — a death that would drain away the specialness from my special place, a death that would leave a crater in the part of my life where a father should be.

The new house was built from lumber recovered from a partially burned house nearby. It was a modest ranch-style house with a covered carport. Jed painted it buttercup yellow with brown shutters, and my grandmother decorated the yard by stabbing synthetic flowers into the soil among real ones in the centers of discarded tires repurposed as flower beds.

The house was a stone's throw from Jed and Big Mama's other house, down a dirt road on the other side of the highway, set on a small parcel notched out of a white farmer's field. It was directly across the road from a kind old widow who had a sprawling yard with a pomegranate tree on one side, its branches straining from the weight of the fruit, and a field on the other side, where Jed and Big Mama grew cucumbers to be sold at the market. There was a butane tank in the yard for fuel, and pungent, metallic-tasting water was drawn from the well in the yard of the widow woman across the street.

The dirt road led into the Bend, a backwater of black families sandwiched between the highway and a bend in the Red River. The Bend had been homesteaded by ex-slaves after the Emancipation Proclamation. When the man who had enslaved them died, his son deeded the ex-slaves that part of the plantation, about a hundred acres.

The families who lived there, many of them direct descendants of those slaves, were tightly bonded but widely scattered — connected by the meandering dirt road and a stubborn devotion to the land that flanked it. We drove into the Bend almost every time we visited — through lush valleys and across wooden bridges spanning rippling brooks, some full of fallen branches, some teeming with cottonmouth snakes. In other spots, the road formed a virtual tunnel through the overgrown leafy canopy. Traffic was so rare in these parts that whenever we came upon a house, which could be miles from its neighbor, everyone in the yard would stop, stand, and wave.

We sometimes drove to the Red River, where we took the ferry to the other side and back again for the sheer slow-motion thrill of it. We stopped at roadside tangles of blackberry bushes or thickets of wild plum trees and gorged ourselves to the point of sickness.

We visited good-natured boys with the quiet charm of people shielded from the world. We visited pretty girls with pretty skin, made so by yard play, homegrown food, and constant sweating. Everywhere we stopped, people came out smiling, genuinely happy to see us, particularly James, whose name they always said in whole, as if it were one word — Jame'Blow — without the *s,* the way folks in Gibsland said Char'esBaby without the *l,* all stretched out like the first notes of a favorite song.

Everyone took to James that way.

In fact, when we visited I didn't get much time with James because everyone else was doting on him. My two oldest brothers seemed to idolize him even though he was younger. William clung to him like a treasured thing once lost but now found. They had been born only nine months apart — Irish twins.

So in Kiblah I often played alone, which I enjoyed, lining up the menagerie of finger-length ceramic animals my grandmother collected on a bric-a-brac shelf, talking to the animals and pretending they talked back to me. The moment that would slice my life into two parts — before and after — was still several years away, but already I was slipping into the isolation that would prime me for it.

About twice a year we'd visit my mother's father, Grandpa Bill, in Houston. He was a handsome, gregarious man — showy but genial — with a broad, toothy smile that forever pinched a half-smoked cigar.

Grandpa Bill was Big Mama's first husband. They had married on Valentine's Day in 1942, a month and a half after the bombing of Pearl Harbor. Big Mama got pregnant with my mother right away, but before she was born Grandpa Bill joined the army, serving in the 92nd Infantry Division, the so-called Buffalo Soldiers. His division was eventually whisked off to Italy, becoming the only all-black division to see combat on the ground in Europe. Grandpa Bill never spoke of his service, but *Buffalo Soldiers in Italy: Black Americans in World War II* recounts Grandpa Bill's valor:

> On 16 November, while proceeding towards the front at night, Sergeant Rhodes's motorized patrol was advanced upon near a village by a lone enemy soldier. Sergeant Rhodes jumped from the truck and as a group of enemy soldiers suddenly appeared, intent upon capturing the truck and patrol intact, he opened fire from his exposed position on the road. His fire forced the enemy to scatter while the patrol dismounted and took cover with light casualties. Sergeant Rhodes then moved toward a nearby building where, still exposed, his fire on the enemy was responsible for the successful evacuation of the wounded patrol members by newly arrived medical personnel. Sergeant Rhodes was then hit by enemy shell fragments, but in spite of his wounds he exhausted his own supply of ammunition then obtaining an enemy automatic weapon, exhausted its supply inflicting three certain casualties on the enemy. He spent the

rest of the night in a nearby field and returned, unaided, to his unit the next afternoon.

Rhodes was Grandpa Bill's family name.

He was the first among the Buffalo Soldiers to be recommended for a Distinguished Service Cross, according to surviving records. That recommendation was declined, like all the recommendations for the Buffalo Soldiers. But his bravery and his injury did earn him a Purple Heart, a Silver Star, an honorable discharge, and a lifelong limp.

When he came home from the war, he and Big Mama made a go of it for a while, first in Louisiana, then in Houston. But after they broke up and got a divorce, Grandpa Bill stayed on in Houston. He married a strikingly beautiful woman only a few years older than my mother who was a bit rough around the edges. They had two daughters, about the ages of my oldest brothers, daughters that my mother could never quite bring herself to call her sisters.

When I was growing up, Grandpa Bill's family lived in a small brick house on a cul-de-sac in a working-class neighborhood in northeast Houston. A large black velvet painting of a curvaceous woman, kneeling with her hands in her hair, breasts exposed, nipples erect, hung in their living room. It looked to me like a painting of Grandpa Bill's young wife, but I dared not ask.

The entire house seemed to be charged with eroticism and wantonness. Grandpa Bill and his pretty young bride openly gambled and drank. Handguns were on display. Porn magazines and condoms were hidden under my grandfather's bed. It was as far from Gibsland — in every way — as I had ever been.

One day when we were visiting, Grandpa Bill was playing a small-money card game in the open garage with a neighbor from across the street. My brothers, our young aunts, and I were playing in the driveway. My grandfather accused the man of cheating. The minor disagreement quickly escalated, fueled by alcohol and my grandfather's sense of honor. My grandfather disappeared into the house and returned with his pistol cocked and aimed. My mother, hysterical, wrestled it away. I was shocked and frightened by how a good time had gone so quickly and badly wrong. Grandpa Bill would surely have killed the man that day, us children watching or no.

Grandpa Bill was quick to violence and unafraid of it. He knew the feel of cold steel in his hand and hot lead in his body. He had been shot twice since the war, for playing around with women who didn't belong to him. Still, he survived. He seemed indestructible, but in need of defense. So his pearl-handled pistol was always nearby.

The feeling I got in Houston was the opposite of the feeling I got in Kiblah. The air in Houston was always charged, and an explosion seemed always imminent. In Houston, even when having fun, I was a ball of nerves.

After her pregnancy with me, and the sickness it brought, my mother got back on her feet, and a neighbor got her a job at the poultry plant in the town of Arcadia, eight miles east of Gibsland, where she stood on her feet on a production line all day cutting chickens for next to nothing: seventy-five cents an hour. She put in two years in that pit before getting a secretarial job at the high school in Gibsland.

All my other brothers were already in school, but I was not. So my mother had my great-uncle Paul keep me during the day so that she could work and then go to school in the afternoon.

Uncle Paul was Papa Joe and Mam' Grace's youngest son, a quiet man unable to read or write his own name. He was dark like a wad of half-chewed tobacco, had wide shoulders into which he diffidently tucked his head like a box turtle, and had a large nose, spread wide and pointed down like a raven's tail. Uncle Paul was now near fifty and had failed to leave the nest. He had lived with Papa Joe and Mam' Grace his whole life.

Every morning I'd stand on the car seat, my small arm tenderly draped around my mother's neck as she drove me to Papa Joe's house.

Uncle Paul was my babysitter, but he was also my best friend — I was growing into childhood, and he had never truly left it.

Papa Joe's house was dimly lit and filled with old furniture, dark and heavy, collected over a long life, imbued with memories but devoid of value. Papa Joe was a former moonshine runner, an enterprise that had earned him a stint in prison. Now older, wiser, and more settled, he farmed hogs and chickens. I followed him around as he did his chores — fixing things, slopping hogs, collecting eggs. Now that Mam' Grace was gone, he barely spoke.

One day Papa Joe went out back to get a chicken from the coop for supper, and I blithely followed. He grabbed one by the neck, walked it over to the well-scarred chopping block, pinned its head down, and chopped it off — one swing of an ax, swift and strong. The headless bird sprang from the block and ran around in a spiral, blood spurting from its neck, until it fell lifelessly to the ground. I was horrified. I passed on chicken for a while.

By late morning, Uncle Paul and I began our long walk back to the House with No Steps. Along the way we passed layabout men leaning against muddy trucks parked under favorite shade trees. They checked in every day like it was a job, swigging cheap liquor from twisted paper bags, entertaining themselves with profane ruminations on the world as it passed them by. They cracked wise about other people's problems, even as they secretly wallowed in regret, lying about wrung-out lives they wished they had lived better, saying things like:

"Dat boy thank he somethin'."

"Uh-huh."

"Thank he shittin' in high cotton."

"Sho nuff."

"And look at dat gal."

"Uh-huh."

"Fuckin' everythang walkin', and half of what's standin' still."

"Sho nuff?"

And we passed old women who sat whiling away the days in sag-
ging chairs on rickety porches, thinking backward, looking out through
eyes grown wise from bodies grown frail.

We stopped to visit with some of Uncle Paul's friends and a few
of our relatives. One of Paul's favorites was Sun Buddy, an imposing
hermit with a long beard that tangled beneath his chin like the roots
of a prairie grass. He drew his name from his habit of sitting quietly
in the sun, sucking it up, in much the same way a frog basks on a river
rock. He lived in a rundown house behind a yard filled with chest-high
weeds, a narrow trail winding through them to a front door that was
barely visible from the street. I never went past the weeds or into the
house, and never heard Sun Buddy speak. I played near the street until
Paul came out.

One of my favorites was a distant cousin named Sarah, one of the
only people I knew in town who was my age. She was being raised
by her grandmother, a kindly old woman whom I couldn't imagine
raising her voice, even to call for help. Sarah was nice with me, but
with her grandmother she released sprays of venom, her irritation
in direct proportion to her grandmother's docility. She seemed sub-
consciously to blame her grandmother for the absence of her real
mother.

A favorite of both of ours was Aunt Odessa, a small, loquacious
woman with deeply wrinkled skin and sprigs of gray hair jutting out
every which way. She lived at the crest of a hill around the corner from
Papa Joe's place, in a small three-room house, unpainted, its wooden
planks weathered silver and warped with decay. Her house had no
bathroom, no plumbing, and no gas heating. She retrieved water from
an outside pipe, and bathed in a washtub. She went to the bathroom in
a slop jar and ferried its contents to a spot out back.

Like the houses of many older people in the area, Aunt Odessa's
didn't have a living room. Every room served as a bedroom, a dining room, and a bathroom. The front door opened onto the largest
room, which contained two beds, a couple of straight-backed chairs,

a large wooden trunk, and a wood-burning heater, the only heater in the house. There was another room that I never entered, and a small kitchen. The kitchen, which opened onto the back porch, contained a decades-old refrigerator, her only electrical appliance, and a massive wood-burning stove that she used to cook simple dishes like cornbread and collard greens.

The house was dark and smelled of mothballs and medicine. But it was always clean and orderly — the product of a simple, utilitarian life that produced little clutter. The only oddity was her collection of Wonder Bread bags, knotted into balls and scattered around the kitchen.

Aunt Odessa came to stay with us one winter because she refused to pay to have a blockage cleared from the flue of her heater. Her stay was supposed to be a few days. It turned into a few months. By the end of the stint, her endless, idiosyncratic babblings, which I usually found both fascinating and hysterically funny, had begun to wear on my mother. When she left, my mother vowed that Aunt Odessa would never come back. "That woman'll worry the horns off a goat."

While at our house, Aunt Odessa seemed to enjoy the relatively modern and comfortable — although gravely modest — amenities. She warmed herself by the gas heater and watched endless hours of TV. However, she seemed irrationally resistant to incorporating these comforts into her own home life. When the town finally installed a sewage system, she resisted offers to have a bathroom built onto her house. She finally relented, a bit, and allowed one to be built as a separate structure, in effect an outhouse with plumbing, a few yards from the back porch.

One of her daughters once bought her a black-and-white TV. She watched it, but when it stopped working, she didn't replace it.

I'd always thought that Aunt Odessa's resistance was a product of poverty and prudence, but when she died, I was told that $16,000 in cash was found in the freezer section of her refrigerator, double- and triple-wrapped in Wonder Bread bags.

Eventually, Uncle Paul and I made it back to the House with No Steps and ate a late lunch. Afterward, I went two doors down to the candy lady's house. Every neighborhood had one — a lady who sold candy out of her house for extra money. Ours had fashioned a "store" from her closed-in carport. She cared for her ailing father-in-law, which burned through all of her patience. I'd knock. "Wait a minute!" she'd shoot back, ever annoyed. Soon enough, she'd shuffle into the store, always in a loose, ankle-length housedress, and unlatch the screen door. "What you want?" She knew what I wanted, but she always asked. I got the same thing every day: a snow cone, ten cents, and five sugar cookies, three cents each. A quarter.

Paul and I spent the rest of the afternoon sitting and talking with the old folks in the neighborhood on their porches. For me it was transcendent.

I was a quiet, introspective boy, and these folks helped me to appreciate that part of myself. They taught me how to be patient and kind — that there was beauty in all things. I picked up their skill for slowing time to a crawl, a skill that people whose time on earth was coming to an end had learned to master. They taught me that you only live once, but for a life well lived, one turn is enough. They baptized me in their sea of stillness, and I emerged more like them than not.

In my kindergarten year, as the holidays approached, Papa Joe died of a stroke and loneliness. At the same time, my parents' marriage was dying of divergent dreams and weariness.

The beginning of the end came one night when my father arrived home late, again, barely beating the sun. My mother was waiting up for him. She had suffered through his controlling nature and his loose ways, but as the old folks had taught me, for everything there comes an end. Cold winters, high fevers, fragile marriages — they all eventually break.

Earlier in their marriage, when I was living in Arkansas, he had worked construction jobs in Houston, and she and my brothers holed up in a single room of Papa Joe and Mam' Grace's house. My mother had tolerated the fact that he had forbidden her to drive the cars he left parked in the yard. When she could find work, she had to bum a ride.

She had tolerated his boorish behavior, the way he leaned against a doorjamb and moved up and down to scratch his back, the way a bear scratches its back against a tree. Things like that set my mother's teeth on edge. My father laughed off her annoyance, as he did most things.

She had tolerated the house he rented with his band, the one where they practiced for gigs and entertained wild women. It was on Boogie Woogie Road.

My mother dealt with my father's women who had the nerve to come to our house. She once came home from working a shift at the chicken plant and found a woman leaving the house. She scrambled to find a brick, which she sent flying through the back window of the woman's car as she drove off.

She had even tolerated having to take armfuls of groceries and armfuls of babies around to the back door because he hadn't built those damned steps. Building the steps would have been such a simple thing. He could have done it. He should have done it. The not-doing spoke volumes.

She had put up with it all, but something about that night was different. Something had changed.

For one thing, she'd left the chicken plant far behind. She'd taken all the classes she needed for her degree to become a home economics teacher. She once told me that she saw teaching as a way out, insurance that she would never end up in a white man's field or a white woman's kitchen. When I was born she was a college dropout still a few credits short of a degree. Now she had that degree, and the year I was five years old she landed a teaching job at the high school in Ringgold, thirty miles southwest of town, where she had done her student teaching.

As part of her studies, and then as part of her new job, she made things: practical things like most of her clothes and some of our furnishings, and magical things like the only stuffed animal I ever got. It was a furry brown dog with floppy leather ears and big button eyes. But it was more than that. It also was the first thing that made me realize that she thought about me when she wasn't looking after me, a realization that sent waves of joy washing over me and made me squeeze the dog so hard that I nearly popped the stitching.

She now had options. She no longer had to put up with my father's behavior. The fever — and the marriage — had broken.

So she sat there in the dark and the silence that night, waiting for him.

He came in, and she let loose. This was bigger than just this one evening. The noise woke us. As it grew louder and more agitated, my brothers and I crept into the hallway, peeking around the corner, a mass of scrawny brown limbs sprouting like weeds in all directions.

My father was drunk and my mother belligerent. This was not going to end well. He grabbed my mother's arms, threw her down onto the sofa, and threw himself on top of her. Something about him didn't seem angry or aggressive to me, but mockingly dismissive, trying to bring a shrill wife to heel. But his attempts to dismiss her anger only seemed to inflame it.

I stole away to the kitchen, grabbed a knife, and ran back to our crouching position in the hallway. My small hand clung desperately to the wooden handle as the heavy blade dangled down to my knee.

I didn't know why I had the knife. I didn't know what I planned to do with it. I was only five years old. All I knew was that I was overcome by fear and anger and sadness, and if I had to choose a side, I was choosing hers. I was a mama's boy — the kind who followed her wherever she went, funerals and all; the kind who always saw her way as right; the kind who shooed away the curious hogs that put their tongues to her hair.

Then my mother cocked her ample legs under his body like the hammer of a gun, thrust them upward, and sent him flying backward, partially through the living room's picture window. He stretched his arms wide and clung to the yellow brocade curtains on either side, keeping himself from tumbling out of the house and onto the broken glass beneath him in the yard. I was relieved, but my mother was still irate. "Let go my damn curtain!" She had made them, too.

In that moment, the power in their relationship shifted, in my mind, from him to her: she was strong, he was weak.

The next morning, my father quietly patched up the window as we left for school. That's the last memory I have of us all together in that house.

Fed up and with a burgeoning career, my mother felt the time had come for a decision: we were leaving my father and moving into Papa Joe's house to live with Uncle Paul. Paul couldn't live alone, and my parents could no longer live together.

During Christmas break Jed and Big Mama came from Kiblah to help us load our things into Jed's truck and began to ferry them across town to our new home, the same old house where I spent most of my mornings, Papa Joe's house, a house with solid steps, steps of brick covered in concrete.

We were still at the House with No Steps, which was nearly empty, on Christmas Eve when Big Mama called from Papa Joe's house and said that Santa had delivered our presents there by mistake. We ran out, jumped on our bikes, and sped through the cold, dark streets as my mother trailed us in the car. We never went back to the House with No Steps again.

At Papa Joe's house, Paul kept the room he'd always had, my mother took Papa Joe's room, and William and Robert took the room in the middle of the house. That left Nathan and me with the room where Mam' Grace had died, our bed pointing in the same direction as her hospital bed had been, facing the picture window. We tried our best to reclaim that room from what had happened in it, but loss still lingered there in the echoes of screams and the memories of tears.

My dad also left the House with No Steps, moving back to his family homestead in Bienville, a small town twenty miles southeast of Gibsland, to stay with his two half-sisters and their husbands in a run-down former bed-and-breakfast just off the highway.

We left our little house with only a month left on the rent-to-own contract. Even one more month would have been too long. My mother had to leave that house to find her way back home.

For my mother, Papa Joe's house was home. She had spent much of her life in that house. She had stayed there as a young girl during the times Big Mama had married and moved away and my mother had refused to follow. She stayed there through college, what she'd finished of it, and even through marriage, occupying one room with my brothers while my father went away to Houston. She left Papa Joe's house only when my father came back to Gibsland from Houston and she moved with us into the House with No Steps.

I thought Papa Joe's house would feel like home to me too, that the move would be easy. But I was wrong. For me, the move was hard. It took me away from the neighborhood that had nurtured me, my village, the place where I was everybody's baby, Char'esBaby, where old folks slowed time to a crawl and a smiling round woman always wanted sugar from Chocolate.

The move plopped me down in the middle of an emotional nothingness, where ever-active bodies with ever-present anxieties moved around and past me the way a stampede moves around and past a stump — like I was barely there.

And my brothers, they didn't seem to have time for me.

Nathan and I still shared a room, but also an unbridgeable developmental divide: I was new to kindergarten, he was newly a teenager. He was almost never home — always out cutting up and chasing girls — and when he was home, there was little for us to talk about.

Many evenings there was no one in our room but me and the memory of Mam' Grace. And, as it had been in the House with No Steps, the only television was in William and Robert's room, where the family still gathered to watch, resting on the bed or on a hand-me-down sofa that my mother had squeezed into the room.

William and Robert shared a special bond that only seemed to grow stronger after my parents split. It was a bond that didn't seem able to stretch wide enough to truly include me or anyone else. I stayed in their room as much as possible, but some part of me always felt like an interloper.

The most fun I had with them was on our rides to school when the three of us were still in the elementary school together. My mother left early every morning for her long drive to work, so we all piled onto William's pieced-together bicycle for the crosstown ride to school — Robert on the seat, me dangling from the handlebars, and William standing, legs pumping the pedals like pistons. We raced along narrow streets, down steep hills, and around blind curves, my face outstretched, eyes closed, parting the dewy air like a hood ornament. It was exhilarating, until one day my heel slipped into the spokes, which removed my shoe and scraped all the skin from the back of my foot. From then on, I approached the rides with trepidation.

As for my mother, she became so consumed with taking care of us that it partially stole her from us. She now had to care for four boys and Uncle Paul, a man-child, all by herself and on her meager salary. At the end of the long days, she'd plop down on her bed, exhausted, and read the newspaper, the *Shreveport Times,* front to back. In fact, no matter how hard we had it, the home delivery of the newspaper was the one thing that she never forswore. I learned early, from her, to love newspapers. Once a week the newspaper came with a Mini Page, a page of news and games designed for children. My mother would save it for me, and I would read my page as she read hers, each of us lost in broad sheets of paper. When my mother wasn't reading, she'd talk on the phone with the gossips until sleep came.

I had never really known the feel of loneliness, but now it was fused to me, creeping up me, the way the kudzu beside the road to Big Mama's house quickly overgrew the trees, encased them in shadows, and choked them to death.

It wasn't a physical loneliness as much as an emotional, spiritual loneliness, a need to be seen and hugged and kissed and held. It was a need to be told stories and have someone listen patiently as I asked too many questions. It was a need to laugh until I cried, about nothing, silly things, with someone who made me feel that I was everything.

No one seemed to notice this need in me, and I was too young and ashamed of it to articulate it. I was so lonely in that house that the first Christmas there I asked for a ventriloquist's puppet — a white boy with red hair and brown freckles whom I tried to make black with a Magic Marker — just so I would have someone to talk to.

I wanted to go back to the House with No Steps, to be among the people who doted on me. It was only a few blocks away. But, for a small child, a few blocks away is a whole world away. I couldn't get there on my own. That place was now lost to me.

At the House with No Steps I had not sensed our shortness of money, but now it was all too apparent. We hadn't been well-off before, but now we would truly struggle.

Most of the blacks in town lived in some gradation of poverty — some barely eking out an existence, some whose existence could hardly be called living. "Poor as Job's turkey," my mother called it.

They were the kind of folks who did hard jobs and odd jobs — any work they could find to keep the lights on and the children fed.

They were women whose skin glistened from steam and sweat, whose hands stayed damp from being dipped in buckets and dried on aprons. They were men who worked in boots with steel toes, the kind that didn't take shining, the kind that leaned over and told stories when you took them off.

They were people whose bodies melted every night in a hot bath, then stiffened by sunrise, so much so that it took pills to get them out of bed without pain.

Yet they seemed to me content in what they knew life to be — sharing old stories, deep laughs, and sweet tea. As the old folks had imparted to me early on, grandeur never witnessed could not be coveted.

Now we were moving to the more desperate end of that spectrum.

My brothers and I spent many Saturdays scavenging at the city dump. It was on the black side of town, just off the elbow of a blind curve, near the highest point of Boogie Woogie Road.

At the dump we combed through the discards of other people's lives, looking for things that could enrich our own, things whose original purpose had expired, things that begged our imaginations to reincarnate them with another. One-rimmed bicycles, card-bare board games, three-legged tables, all dug from rippling heaps under the glare of hungry dogs.

Being a child with nothing, it didn't take much to satisfy me. The smallest trinkets sparked the wonder of great treasure — a copper penny, a gold button, a fake gem wiggled free from fake jewelry. They were ideas made real in faraway places by unknown hands, things that somehow made their way into mine, things that, when touched, connected me to another world, one I thought I might never see, where people might have time for me.

I filled my pockets with these things — talismans against tough times, reminders that the world was bigger than what I saw.

But even at the junkyard, even with my brothers there, I still found myself alone. They ventured deep into the garbage while I scavenged in heaps close to the street, in case we had to run from the dogs.

I was tense around dogs. One had almost killed me when we lived in the House with No Steps. I had gone to play one afternoon with other children at the Methodist church down the street, its asphalt-and-gravel parking lot doubling as a scar-multiplying playground. I stood savoring a bottle of soda. It was a rare treat, so I took my time, paying attention to every swig, sliding my tongue into the opening until bubbles burned the taste buds on the tip.

At the time, my mother was chatting with her friends in an adjacent house, trading gossip and giggles, talking as they did about half-a-husbands and a whole lot of problems, propping each other up so that life wouldn't wear them down.

One of the neighborhood dogs, a German shepherd named King, weaved a path among us children, panting in the heat. He stopped with his back to me, his fluffy tail rocking back and forth in slow motion. I extended my hand and gently grabbed it. That was my mistake. King turned, fangs bared, and attacked — his hulking frame pinning my small one to the ground. As I lay on my back, he lunged for my face. His eyes went blank. The King I knew was no longer inside that animal.

I instinctively grabbed his throat with my free hand and held him off with an arm made stiff by sheer terror. With the other hand I held the soda out from the commotion, upright so that it wouldn't spill. Two hands would have been better to keep myself from being mauled, but my brain didn't make that click. That was my soda, and I intended to finish it.

The other children screamed for the mothers, and the mothers burst out of the house, yelling and screaming with the emphasis and pitch only mothers can produce when a child is in danger.

They scared King away, but not before he carved a wound deep into the part of me that trusted things. I would especially never trust another dog that didn't belong to us, let alone a rib-bare, junkyard dog scrounging for scraps.

When my brothers and I finished our digging in the junkyard, we climbed into the ditch across the street and dug for a treat. We flaked off pieces of edible clay dirt that smelled to me like dry earth at the beginning of a fresh rain and tasted like chalk soaked in vinegar. Folks said it was good for you. Settled your stomach. Staved off illness. All

I knew was the taste was addictive, and that ditch — where the curve of the road cut deep into the ground and exposed the strata — was the only place in town where that dirt could be found. Best of all, it was free.

In my family's new life, the most pressing need was to make sure that we stayed fed, so most of our time and energy went into the growing, picking, and preparing of food.

Luckily, the house was set on two acres of land strewn with fruit trees — crab apple trees to the right, peach trees behind, fig and plum trees across the street. Another tree out back rained pecans in the fall, and blackberries sprouted up along the fencerow every other summer. We munched on fruit and nuts all day. Whatever we picked in abundance my mother baked into thick-crusted cobblers or bubbling pies.

We grew our own vegetables across the road. The paved street in front of the house had been laid without regard for property lines, sometimes leaving thin slivers of people's property across the road from their houses. Some folks did nothing with these scraps of land. Others used them for parking. We turned ours into two truck patch gardens, each about five yards across and fifteen yards long, lying on either side of a small abandoned house that Papa Joe used to rent out to make extra money.

In the spring, an old man with a mule-drawn plow came to turn the earth. I watched as the man and the mule yanked and pulled each other across the fields, to a chorus of giddyaps and winnies and whoas, until they had created wobbly rows of corrugated soil — crumbly, nearly black, alive with bugs and worms. It smelled strongly of humus, a smell that reached down to the core of me.

We planted a couple rows of purple hull peas, a couple rows of corn, a half row of tomatoes, and a half row of green beans. Then we planted a couple hills of cucumber and onion on part of the back row. On the rest of the back row my mother let me plant whatever I liked. I chose watermelon, but I didn't have the patience to let them ripen.

When they got to be football-sized I picked them, although the flesh was invariably still white.

Gardening taught me things I didn't even know I was learning — lessons about patience and caretaking, but most important about disturbance as a condition of growth, that solid ground had to be plowed up for new seeds to take root.

When harvest time came, we stayed in the fields all day, picking as much corn and as many peas or beans or greens as we could, trying not to leave a thing.

At night we sat in a circle, around a mound of vegetables atop an old sheet on the floor in the middle of the room, each person with a large pan, and shucked corn, or snapped green beans, or shelled peas until our fingers turned dark from the pods. We would watch television, tell family stories, and laugh until we nearly peed our pants.

Everything had to be canned or frozen for the lean winter months. We poured cucumbers, sweet and pickled, and jams and preserves into Mason jars, which we sealed in large shallow pans of slow-boiling water. Blanched peas and tomatoes, cob-scraped corn, and garden vegetable soups we ladled into plastic bags to be frozen.

Shelling peas and canning pickles: these were the times that drew us together, the only times when I didn't feel alone in that house. But harvest season lasted only a season. Soon it was done, and I shifted back into the shadows.

Another occasion that drew us together and made me feel I served a function in our family was Hog Killing Day.

We used a small space behind the house, beyond the clothesline and under the pecan tree, to raise a couple of hogs, while the large field, where Papa Joe had raised hogs, grew verdant with tall weeds.

We fattened the hogs until it was time to kill them. It was always after the first frost, after the flies were gone and wouldn't get at the meat. On that day, the hog killers came before daybreak. They were a small group of old men who still knew how to kill a hog right. They knew where the joints were, how to get through the cartilage, how to get butchers' cuts from whole slabs.

We gathered around the pen as one of the men raised a rifle. He wanted a direct shot to the head, but that didn't always happen. When the bullet hit elsewhere, the hog unleashed a hell-raising squeal.

When the hog went down the throat was cut, to let it bleed out. Then it was dipped in a barrel of boiling water to remove the hair, after which its hind legs were hooked to a crossbar and its body was pulled up the pecan tree.

The carcass was split neck to nuts, and the innards were scooped out. They weren't bloody, but shiny like jewelry — rose quartz and pale amethyst and pearly white. The head was sawed off and set aside for hog head cheese, and the hide was peeled away for cracklings.

That was my job: cooking the cracklings. The sheets of skin were cut into small chunks, tossed into a cast-iron caldron that was half as deep as I was tall, and heated on all sides by a log fire. I stirred them around with the stick-end of a used-up broom until the fat melted and the pieces crackled in the oil they made. The cracklings were scooped out, salted, and eaten right away, so hot that they burned the tongue, so tasty that we didn't care.

But Hog Killing Day lasted just a day. When the killing and the carving and the cooking of the cracklings were done, the old men were paid in meat and money and disappeared in their old trucks. And my loneliness came back home.

The house had a small galley kitchen where my mother performed daily miracles, stretching a handful into a potful, making the most of what we raised.

Cooking mostly from memory and instinct, she took a packet of meat, a bunch of greens or a bag of peas, a couple of potatoes, a bowl of flour, a cup of cornmeal, a few tablespoons of sugar, added a smattering of this and a smidgeon of that, and produced meals of rich and complementary flavors and textures. Delicious fried chicken, pork chops, and steak, sometimes smothered with hearty gravy, the meat so tender that it fell from the bone.

Cob-scraped corn pan-fried in bacon drippings, served with black-eyed peas and garnished with thick slices of fresh tomato, a handful of diced onion, and a tablespoon of sweet pickle relish.

A mess of overcooked turnips simmering in neck-bone-seasoned pot liquor, nearly black — tender and delectable. The greens were minced on the plate, doused with hot pepper sauce, and served with a couple sticks of green onions and palm-sized pieces of hot-water cornbread, fried golden brown, covered with ridges from the hand that formed them, crispy shell, crumbly soft beneath.

Mam' Grace had taught my mother how to turn scrap meat into whole meals. Chicken backs, necks, and gizzards made aromatic stock for rice or dumplings. Chitlins, hog maws, and tripe were boiled all day or pan-fried, then doused with hot sauce. Boiled pigs' feet were drizzled with vinegar to add some kick and keep our fingers from sticking together when we ate them. Chicken and beef livers were fried crispy and spicy.

And none of the food was to be wasted.

When my mother was coming up, people ate anything and everything just to survive. They ate the whole chicken, even the brain, scrambled in eggs, then cracked the bones and sucked the marrow.

My mother grew up having her hair greased with olive oil and her legs slathered with bacon grease because she couldn't afford body lotion or even a steady supply of petroleum jelly. She cleaned her teeth with a rag dipped in a solution of baking soda and salt because she couldn't afford toothpaste or a brush. She slept in a ratty-dress-turned-nightgown between a handmade quilt and sheets stitched from old sacks. She drank tea made from cow chips and pine needles to ward off a cold because her family couldn't afford medicine. Waste was unconscionable for those who had grown up with barely enough, and we now had to lean on that learning more than ever.

If anything was left on your plate, you were scolded: "Yo' eyes bigga than yo' belly!"

And no food was to be tossed because of bruising or the onset of decay. There was always another way to use something. Bread ends and stale scraps were crumbled and baked into a bread pudding. Dark spots on rotting bananas were carved out, the remains sliced thin and layered into banana pudding. Bruised spots were pared from apples, the good parts chopped up, dusted with cinnamon and sugar, folded into pockets of dough, and pan-fried until golden brown. Half-sour milk was used to make biscuits and bread, a dash of baking soda added to cut the acid.

When something truly spoiled, it became scraps for the dogs or was dropped into the slop bucket for the hogs.

When the weather got warm enough we fished, as much because we needed to as we wanted to. We fished anywhere you could get a bite — lakes and reservoirs, streams and rivers, spillways and ditches, natural and man-made ponds. All we needed was a pole or rod, a can of worms dug from a shady spot in the yard, and a bucket for the catch. We found a favorable bend in the bank, a spot where weeds were worn down by foot traffic, and moved as close to the water as we could without slipping in. I liked to get close enough to catch sight of the swarms of minnows or clouds of tadpoles playing in the safety of the shallows.

We'd often clean and fry our catch on the same day — palm-sized perch, largemouth bass, and flathead catfish (my favorite) — their cornmeal-encrusted tails arching upward from the hot oil. We served them with a side of home fries and a vinegar-splashed salad of lettuce, tomatoes, and cucumbers.

But no matter how hard we worked and how much we scrimped, we couldn't seem to escape the specter of hardship. Not having enough was an ever-present worry, so much so that my mother and her friends took to scavenging the wreckage of cargo trucks that overturned on the interstate.

One truck accident happened on a spring night shortly after we'd moved into Papa Joe's house. The air was richly scented with fresh pine and new flowers and laced with a slight chill and endless possibilities.

My brothers and I were huddled around the front door with its solid steps. A single exposed bulb sprayed us with harsh light, bands of it passing between our legs and bodies and streaking across the yard. My brothers kicked the dirt and threw rocks into the nothingness, longing for something more to do, constrained by the reality that our tiny town went to sleep when night fell. So they were doing what they often did — talking about hopes, dreams, and what-ifs, imagining lives much better than our own, dreaming of a world in which they were the center.

I tuned it all out, instead concentrating on the small drama playing out just above our heads.

The light attracted a steady stream of lazy brown bugs the size and shape of half a small grape cut lengthwise. I marveled at the aggressive spiders that sprang from the voids in the siding to seize the bugs that had the misfortune of setting their webs atremble. The spiders made swift business of their prey. They were brutal, unforgiving, hell-bent on survival, like everything else in my world.

Inside, my mother and grandmother, who was visiting from Arkansas, sat at the dining table cutting geometric shapes from old clothes to make new quilts, stacking each shape and color with its kind to create little fabric towers with jagged edges. They bickered, as they usually did, about minor things, nothing really. It was their way of relating to each other, of loving each other.

The phone rang. My mother answered. The voice on the other end screamed with joy that a cattle truck had overturned on the interstate and the wounded cows had been left behind.

Interstate 20 was less than a mile north of town. When cargo trucks wrecked near our exit, the phones lit up, and off we went to scour what was left. In the past it had been paper towels or onions or potatoes. This night it was meat. Jackpot!

This was what scared me about the night: the darkness and the mystery, the way things could suddenly shift, the way it turned people, changed them, the way it gave cover for things not done in the glare of daylight, things that would go unmentioned when the sun came up.

Even in my enchanted Kiblah I shrank in fear from the darkness. There the night seemed to fall three shades darker than anywhere else in the world, and the sky — velvet black and studded with more stars than there were wishes — seemed two times bigger. Even there the shadows seemed to move and things came out of them, things like the erratic bats that picked off the bugs attracted to the light on the telephone pole in front of the little yellow house.

But I was more scared of what else might move out of those shadows, like the monster that walked like a person. Folks talked convincingly about a Bigfoot that stalked those parts at night. There was even a movie made about it: *The Legend of Boggy Creek,* a creek just up the road from Kiblah. It was a docudrama, with people giving eyewitness accounts of a creature that bayed at the moon, tracked through folks' bean fields, and killed their cows. The film opened with a narrator gravely saying of the monster, "I was seven years old when I first heard him scream. It scared me then, and it scares me now." All the talk of "it" scared me too. Every time I looked out a window at night, I was afraid I might see eyes looking back at me.

That night when the truck overturned, the darkness overtook us and we became the things stalking the night to kill the cows. Our house came alive with excitement as we scrambled for coats and keys and rifles. We quickly loaded into the two cars — I into the car that one of my brothers drove while another rode shotgun, and everyone else in the other car.

We drove silently, tense with anticipation.

We entered the interstate in the eastbound lanes and slowly passed the spot where the wreckage had been, marked by scarred asphalt and littered with debris. Stunned and wounded cows limped into the traffic, the median, and the bordering woods. We went about a mile up the road to survey the whole scene, crossed the median, and started back down the westbound lanes.

As the car slowed, my brother hoisted himself partway out the open window with the rifle. He took aim, and, with a single shot, a huge cow fell. The sound of the shot was diffused by the traffic, but not completely muffled. The crew in the other car also bagged a cow.

A man with a pulpwood truck, whom my mother had called before we left home, helped load the dead animals into the trunks of the cars as best they could fit. We drove fifteen miles through winding back roads to the house of one of Paul's brothers, a tall, gentle man who was the deacon of a Methodist church and an amateur chicken farmer. He and his wife — a short, melancholy woman with a raspy voice and a thick mustache — lived there with their children at the bottom of a tall hill. The house was half a mile from the main road and at least half a mile from the nearest neighbor.

I fell asleep on the way. When I woke I realized that the car was parked and I was the only person in it, alone again. I raised myself so that I could see through the windshield. One of the disemboweled animals' bodies was hanging by its hind legs from a tree by the side of the house — its bloody entrails sliced from their cavity and spilled beneath it, steamy in the cold predawn air. My family worked feverishly, carving flesh and ferrying pink-marbled slabs of it into the house, visibly elated by the clandestine enterprise and the good fortune that had befallen us. They whispered terse instructions, quietly celebrated their progress, and moved with the speed and caution of a team of surgeons — racing against time, which would soon bring daylight and unwanted attention.

The area was lit by headlights that cast long shadows trailing off into the darkness. The scene dimmed as my eyelids fell, heavy with the exhaustion of having seen too much.

While outright stealing was unacceptable, in my mother's view, opportunistic scavenging was simply an act of survival. She was wedged between two uncompromising positions. On the one hand was her absolute refusal of, and disdain for, the charity of others, particularly government welfare — she often seethed about a local woman with a brood of children who had once boasted of being able to make more money taking welfare than other women could make putting in an honest day's work. On the other hand was my mother's stubborn determination to show the world, and perhaps herself, that she was strong enough to make it on her own.

But my mother was adamant that we would not suffer in the process. Nothing stirred her spirit or shielded her guilt like a child's wide-eyed gaze of worry, the voicing of a need she could not meet, or the terrible rumble of a tiny stomach she could not fill. Hunger isn't only the great motivator, it's the great stealer of joy. The very idea of it moved my mother to make sure that our joy was protected from it.

So, like the spiders in the cracks, she sprang at every scrap of good fortune. The only way that she could see to make ends meet was to stretch the rules that bound them. Why let those wounded cows wander into the woods, die, and be pecked clean by buzzards when we were in such need? She wasn't proud of scavenging, but she refused to be ashamed of doing everything in her power to ensure that we would never see a hungry day. We never did.

2

Thanksgiving

The only time I ever saw a person actually shoot a gun at another, I was five years old, and it was my mother shooting at my father.

It was the summer after they'd separated. He'd slept over the night before. I had crept into her bed, as I often did, and fallen back to sleep. But soon the rustling woke me. I looked over to see my father on top of her. They were staring into each other's eyes, intently, silently, seemingly saying things without words.

I now thought that getting into her bed had been a bad idea. I didn't know what was happening, but I figured that it wasn't for my eyes to see, so I closed them and pretended to be still asleep.

I didn't understand what was going on, but I did understand that my mother's new life in Papa Joe's old house was the first time I saw her as a whole person, separate from a man, independent. It wasn't a grand life or an easy one, but it was hers. She lived it in miniature — celebrating small accomplishments, counting small blessings, stretching small money, avenging small slights. I was coming to recognize that she took some measure of pride in her hard-won self-reliance.

So her being in bed with my father, whom I was increasingly coming to view as less than whole, confused me.

She occasionally let him sleep over, which I read as a weakness. I wasn't old enough to understand the complexities of the heart and the vulnerabilities of the flesh. My mother was a woman like any other, who sometimes must have needed the comfort of a man, even that man, to hold her tight, to make her feel beautiful, loved, and protected.

The next morning, my mother sprang up, moving happily about, making breakfast. In the bed I stared at my father as he slept, trying to figure out what he had done to her, what those things were that he had said to her with his eyes, those things that didn't need words.

Around midmorning, a young boy called and asked to speak to my father. It was a boy my mother didn't know, and besides, who knew that my father was here? Suspicious, she woke my father, called him to the phone, then quietly went to the phone in the living room to eavesdrop. She would later tell me what the boy had said: "My mama said meet ha down to West End." West End was a slant-roofed juke joint just off the highway and just outside the city limits, halfway between our street and Boogie Woogie Road. Most nights the place played host to a scraggly lot of tough men and loose women.

I got the sense from my mother — in the things she said under her breath for no one to hear, and in the things I overheard her saying on the phone with the gossips — that she could forgive some of the men who went there. In fact, she seemed to like men with a pinch of devil — not low down, but not uptight. Tilted. Rooted in good but leaning toward trouble. They were the kind with enough respect for home to cover their tracks when they ran the streets. Work-till-they-smell-bad, but clean-up-good men. Do-wrong-sometimes, do-right-most-of-the-time men. Men one step shy of my father.

But she sniffed at women who hung around places like that. They were the ones she waved at but never spoke to. High-heeled, naked-leg women. Too-short-dress and too-much-teeth women. Whistling girls and crowing hens. The lay-down-and-take-up-with-a-man-not-their-own women. The women who went out and slept in, more at home on their backs than on their feet. The drinkers. The ones who wasted money buying a plate of something instead of making a pot of something. Lazy, frivolous, loose — good-time women. Those women. The opposite of her.

My mother never drank or danced. She never partied in any way, let alone at a low-down juke joint. She didn't even follow television, except the news and *Wheel of Fortune* and shows like *Sanford and Son* and *Good Times,* which she watched with us when we shelled peas and shucked corn. She read the newspaper.

She was a do-right woman, not a good-time woman. But now one of *those* women was calling *her* house for *her* husband to come meet *her* at the West End. Too many levels of disrespect.

My mother shrieked. There was a commotion. She went for her pistol.

While my brothers and I, like most boys in those parts, had rifles — small-caliber hand-me-downs used to keep snakes out of the grass and vermin out of the garden, and BB and pellet guns used for target practice and shooting birds for sport — my mother had the only handgun in the house.

It seemed to show up soon after we moved to Papa Joe's house, and like me, it followed her everywhere, tucked in her purse, nestled among peppermints and pencils. It was a business piece with no benign intent, protection for a woman who had inherited her father's, my Grandpa Bill's, warrior spirit, and who was now out in the world on her own.

And she had brass knuckles stashed in the glove box. The gun and the brass knuckles were a guard against women who forgot their place and jumped slick, and against men driven crazy by thirst long after the love had dried up. These were men like the pulpwood cutter, whom she'd made the mistake of dating shortly after leaving my father. Realizing her error, she let him go, but for him letting go was hard to do.

One day on our drive home from Ringgold, he tailgated us for miles, his big truck bearing down on our back bumper. When my mother had had enough, she pulled over, grabbed the pistol, and marched back to confront the man. I turned in my seat to see what would happen. I could make out only snippets of her scolding as she cursed a blue streak, using all the bad words children get spanked for using. The line I remember most was about me:

"Are you crazy? My baby's in that damned car!"

He never bothered us again.

Maybe that was why she had let my father back in: he was comfortable, and for all else he might have been, he wasn't dangerous.

But that morning, after a night of pleasure, a little boy's voice on the other end of a phone had shattered her pride and broken her heart. That morning she grabbed that gun to conduct some business with my father.

He rushed to get dressed, then burst out of the back door clutching his pants at the waist, belt dangling. He bounded down the steps and leapt across the yard and over the fence where my mother had thrown herself when Mam' Grace died. He continued through the tall grass that grew where Papa Joe had raised the hogs, the dewy seed heads lapping at his legs as he tried to make it to the woods beyond the fence on the other side.

My mother flung the door open behind him, her gun in hand, and began firing — her shots pierced the morning silence, but missed my father. I watched from my mother's bedroom window as my father flinched at each explosion. But there was something in his gait that did not suggest a man whose life was in danger, but rather a rascally boy who'd been caught being devilish. It was a casual quickness, not flat-out running, that pushed him across the field, something in him that knew that something in her wouldn't do it.

Maybe that's what drew a smile on my face, the idea that there was a smile on his, too, even when his pants got caught in the barbed wire of the second fence as he tried to clear it. My mother ran to her car and canvassed the neighborhood for him, but to no avail. We found out later that he had hidden in a neighbor's house.

Shooting a cheating husband was not uncommon. It was a thing often done. In fact, one of my mother's best friends had shot her husband a couple years before for the same reason.

The woman had full hips, high cheekbones, and a short fuse. She lived in a tiny house with her husband and their four children over a hill from the House with No Steps. The husband was the blackest person I'd ever seen. A magnificent, unreal blackness. Burnt black. Shiny. Obsidian. Almost iridescent, the way the light danced across his skin, like the feathers left by the flock of black birds that blotted out the sun and set down in our backyard every winter on their way south, like our house was a place on a map.

The way folks told it, the full-hipped wife found out that her burnt-black husband was cheating with a younger woman who was known to lie down under older men. So one night, as the man sat watching television with the children, his wife stepped from the bedroom, drew her gun, and aimed at the back of his head. The children screamed. The man jumped and turned. The bullet meant for his head caught him in the stomach. As he lay bleeding out his black belly like a stuck hog, she dressed the children and took them to the Webster Parish Fair in Minden, a town fifteen miles west of Gibsland, leaving the man to die while folks munched on cotton candy and plucked numbered plastic ducks from a false stream.

Infidelity was license to kill. There was a bullet or a knife or a kettle of boiling water or a pot of hot grits waiting for any lover who dared lay up with a "Jody" or a "Clean Up Woman." There were people all around who bore the marks of their sins — a chin-strap scar from a cut throat, leathery skin from a scalding, the nub of a shot-off arm. I had learned early in life that the wages of betrayal were meted out at the end of a gun barrel.

No one called the police before a bad thing happened. The police came only after the body fell. And besides, there was just one police officer in town and no real jail, save an abandoned red calaboose, set beside the shallow ditch that divided the town into black and white.

When someone felt wronged, they ignored the code of law and invoked the code of honor, leaving the details for God to sort out later.

In the case of the full-hipped woman, God saw fit to let her husband live.

And God saw fit to let my father live. Or maybe it was just my mother who had seen fit to let him live. Surely she could have hit him, if in fact she was aiming to. The distance was too short, her view too unobstructed. She was a better shot than that for sure. I believe that it was love that blurred her vision and bent the barrel. A heart still works even when it's broken.

So that was it. My mother was done. She had let him back in to lie with her in her new bed, his body making the same old promises, promises that he had no intention of keeping, saying tender, lovely things that could only be passed through the press of flesh and the tips of fingers by a person with whom you shared a past and from whom you'd split apart.

But it seemed to me, even in their language without words, that his body must still have told lies. So many lies. Smooth, easy lies. The kind that fill women's minds like smoke fills a hive. The kind that make women drunk with hope, thick blinding hope, the dangerous kind of hope that makes them lose their grip on good sense.

But no more. Not for my mother. She should have been done the night she kicked him out the window and their marriage shattered, but he patched things up. But what they had could not truly be fixed. It had to be abandoned. He was more trouble than he was worth. He and his lying body. She would be a fool for no man. This was the new, or renewed, mama. The strong mama. My mama. My father never slept over again. In fact, no man did.

After that, she began to talk openly about my father's shortcomings — talking more to herself than to us. Each comment was an affirmation, a reminder, that no matter how hard we now had it, we were better off without him. She reminded us that he never paid his child support — only $25 — although he regularly came to our house with a pocketful of uncashed work checks.

My mother's derision widened the breach between my father and me into a gaping void, filled with the shards of broken promises, atta-boys unspoken, and hugs not given. At the same time, my father sank into alcoholism.

Occasionally, late at night, without warning, the drunken wreckage of him would wash up on our doorstep, stammering, laughing, reeking, voice amplified by the booze.

Bang! Bang! Bang! "Billie, open the do'! These my boys just like they is yourn!"

He was on his way home from drinking, gambling, philandering, or some combination of sins, squandering money that we could have used, wasting time that we desperately needed, sometimes just down the block from our house. As a parting gift, he'd drop by to bless "his boys" with an incoherent thirty minutes of drunken drivel, crumbs from the table of his paternity that I hungrily lapped up, time that would be lost to him in the fog of a hangover by the time day broke. It was as close as I could get to him, so I took it.

He spouted off about what he planned to do for us, buy for us. But the slightest thing we did or said drew the response, "You jus' blew it." We always seemed to blow it. I tried not to blow it *every* time, but no matter how hard I tried: "You jus' blew it." I came to understand that he had no intention of doing anything. The one man who was supposed to be genetically programmed to love me didn't understand what it meant to love a child, or to hurt one.

To him, this was a harmless game that kept us excited and begging. In fact, although I couldn't fully comprehend it at the time, it was a cruel, corrosive deception that subtly and unfairly shifted the onus for his lack of emotional and financial responsibility from him to us.

All I could do was lose faith in his words and in him. I stopped believing. Stopped begging. Stopped expecting. I wanted to stop caring, but I couldn't. A heart still works even when it's broken.

According to the stories folks told, Blow men had always been a grab bag — some hard workers, some hustlers, all smart — all the way back to slavery. My father had a smidgeon of each kind in him. The family traces its roots back to Southampton, Virginia, the same piece of land that produced Nat Turner and Dred Scott, who was actually born Sam Blow. In the early 1800s the man who enslaved Dred moved from Virginia to Alabama with his handful of slaves. That's where my father's family history picked up.

My father's great-grandfather — who, someone told me, was a high-yellow mulatto man with a flowing mane of dirt-red hair — is said to have saved for many years to buy his own freedom, then to buy a few hundred acres to farm along the Coosa River near a town called Wetumpka, an Indian word meaning "rumbling waters," just north of Montgomery.

His oldest child, my father's grandfather, was a tiny man with big ideas named Columbus. The story I heard was that he ran afoul of white folk in Alabama. Some say he hid a ballot box when it appeared that a Klan-backed candidate for sheriff might've won an election. Others say he shot and killed a white man, but few people put much stock in that story. Whatever the case, the Klansmen — "white tops," they called them — were after him. So he fled one night, leaving his young wife — a half-Indian midwife — and their young children behind. He quietly followed the river and its rumbling waters out of town and found his way to a swampy stretch of land two states over and about thirty miles south of Gibsland.

It would be two years before he sent for his family.

The way folks told it, Columbus began sharecropping a large cotton farm there in Louisiana and made a success of it — too much of a success, it turned out. They said that when he had earned enough money to buy the farm outright, the local whites "put a bad white man on him" who harassed and threatened him, and on at least one occasion tried to kill him, shooting into his house while the family was inside. He refused to leave, but his young bride didn't have his fortitude. Fearing for her life and that of her children, she left him. He wanted that farm — he had earned it — but he wanted her more, so he soon left to join her, about ten miles north, near Bienville.

White folks had run him off again, but again he had just started over. According to the stories, he established the first black church in the region, which met under a brush arbor until the congregation could erect a building. He earned a living making wooden caskets and baskets from strips of white oak, and blacksmithing.

Folks spoke of Columbus — or Old Man Blow, as they called him — with a weighty reverence, as a hero, and that's how I saw him: a savvy, courageous man willing to do what he believed was right, even if it meant turning away from everything he knew, a man who always bounced back after having to start over, a man who always chose love.

But Old Man Blow was where the trail of honor ran cold.

My father's father was by all accounts a peculiar man who piddled about. People rarely spoke of him, but what I heard was that he stayed with Columbus most of his adult life, except for the two periods, one early in life and one late, when he was married. He did anything for money but hold on to a real job — selling watermelons or sodas or hiring himself out to people without cars who needed a ride to town. Most of the time when folks talked about him, he was the butt of jokes. I repeatedly heard the story of how he was so cheap that he would drive up a hill, kill the engine at the top, and roll down the other side to save a little gas.

He fathered my father by a woman my mother always described as "the most beautiful dark-skinned woman I have ever seen." The pairing of my peculiar grandfather and my beautiful, dark-skinned grandmother was apparently a violation of the order of things. From what I heard and the pictures I saw, the Blows were so fair of complexion that many could have passed for white. Society sent all kinds of signals, even signals a child like me could register and absorb — that light skin was a precious thing to be perpetuated, not squandered. And that those of us not in possession of it were often devalued to the extent of our deficiency.

Because of the dark skin my father inherited from his mother, and the unpleasant circumstance of his paternity, it seemed to me that my father was literally and figuratively a black sheep of the Blow family. He didn't seem to have much investment in its legacy. I never once heard him speak of his father or Old Man Blow or any of his folks, although I wanted and needed those stories.

But my father said nothing. He stashed those stories away like his guitars: in a dark place where he didn't have to be reminded of them and no one else could hear them.

Maybe it was his own complicated relationship to his father and his father's family that rendered my father cold. Maybe it was being witness to the absence of his siblings' fathers. Maybe it was the pain and guilt of his car accident. Who knows? But whatever it was, it stole him from us. And I had it worse than my brothers.

While my brothers talked ad nauseam about breaking things and fixing things, I spent many evenings reading and wondering. My favorite books from our small collection were the encyclopedias. The volumes were bound in white leather with red writing on the covers. They allowed me to explore the world beyond my world, to travel without leaving home, to dream dreams greater than my life would otherwise have supported. I was new to reading, so I preferred the volumes packed with pictures, like G: gemstones and Ghana, Galileo and gravity. Glorious.

In fact, the first thing that I ever remember buying was a book. It was on one of the days my mother gave me a couple of dollars at Kmart. I ran for the Hot Wheels section. I could afford two: ninety-nine cents each. But on the way, the children's books caught my eye. I stopped and flipped through them until I found one that I wanted: a picture book of Job from the Bible. I would treasure that book the way a boy treasures his first wallet or pocketknife or pellet gun.

But losing myself in my own mind also meant that I was lost to my father.

My father could relate more easily to my brothers' tactile approach to the world than to my cerebral one. He understood the very real sensation of touching things — the weight of a good wrench, the tension of a guitar string, the soft hairs on the nape of a harlot's neck — more than the supernal magic of literature and learning.

So, not understanding me, he simply ignored me, even more than the others — not just emotionally, but physically as well. Never once did he hug me, never once a pat on the back or a hand on the shoulder or a tousling of the hair. I mostly experienced him as a distant form in a heavy fog.

My best memories of him were from his episodic attempts at engagement. During the longest-lasting of these episodes, once every month or two he would come pick us up and drive us a few miles west on Interstate 20 to Trucker's Paradise, a seedy, smoke-filled truck stop with gas pumps, a convenience store, a small dining area, and a game room through a door in the back. It had a few video games, a couple of pinball machines, and a pool table. Perfect.

My dad gave each of us a handful of quarters and we played until they were gone. He sat up front in the dining area, drinking coffee and being particular about the measly food.

"Is this soup fresh or from the cain?!"

We loved those days. To us, Trucker's Paradise *was* paradise. The quarters and the games were fun but easily forgotten. It was the presence of my father that was most treasured. But those trips were short-lived. My father soon sank back into his sewer of booze and women.

And so it was. Every so often he would make some sort of effort, but every time it wouldn't last.

When he wouldn't come to us, my mother would take us to him, trying to keep some connection between a bunch of boys, their father, and his folks. She'd drive us to the house in Bienville where he lived with his two sisters and their husbands.

The house was a U-shaped building that surrounded a grass-bare courtyard with a tree withering in the middle. It had high ceilings and dark rooms, especially the spooky, blood-red-painted bathroom, lit by a single exposed bulb, that scared away my need to pee.

On one side of the house was my father's fast-talking, foulmouthed sister, a woman prone to wild exaggeration and flat-out lying who lived with her mixed-race husband. He had a head of greasy gray hair, straight as strings, although it wasn't really gray, or white, but dingy, like three-day-old snow when the grime and mud and dog piss gets mixed in. He was the preacher without a church who had married my parents under the tree. He ate fried fish whole, bones and all, and liked to tell us about the disgusting ways white people described black people when they mistook him for one of their own, a mistake easily made since there were no discernible echoes of Negro heritage in his appearance.

On the other side of the house lived my father's ever-smiling, dwarfish sister, whose overweight frame sweated like a cold drink in a glass jar. She had the kind of look that the world treats cruelly, the kind that pushes a person to extreme pleasantness or extreme bitterness just to survive it. She chose pleasantness. She lived there with her no-account husband, who rarely worked but always drank, and their fun-loving son, who liked to wrestle and loved to laugh.

My father had a room in the middle, between the two families.

Our visits weren't always warm ones. My father, if he was even home, rarely spoke, and my mother had an uneasy relationship with his sisters. She liked the dwarfish one, but that one kept a nasty house. And the other one was a liar. My mother often reminded us of what my father's mother had said about the lying sister: "She's my daughter, Billie, but she sure can lie." My mother detested liars.

Not all of my father's folks were too keen on my mother either, which they made known when my mother wasn't around. My mother's conservative bent, the way she didn't curse in mixed company, her going back to college as a grown woman with children, none of it seemed to set right with them. To them, such things were the mark of a woman who thought too much of herself. And they couldn't comprehend why my mother had left my father.

What kind of woman strikes out to raise all of us boys on her own? What kind of woman puts a man down just because he's acting up? Surely a piece of a man was better than no man. They reckoned that it was a woman's lot in life to make do with a scrap of a husband if that was what she was given. My mother reckoned differently.

They slyly pleaded my father's case to us boys, but I was the kind of boy who always saw my mother's way as right, so their side-taking soured me on those visits.

As my mother was struggling to keep my real father in my life, Jed, the man I counted as my first father, the one I loved most, was on his way out of it.

Jed fell ill — lung cancer, from a lifetime of smoking. He was in the hospital for a spell but came home when there was no more the doctors could do. He was bedridden, thin, nearly gone. Toward the end, my brother James came to stay with us in Gibsland for a week, but it was not a happy time. Something was wrong. I could feel it. No one said anything, but something came through the silence like the buzz in a too-quiet room: nothing, but something.

The next week, when we took James back to Arkansas, there were strange cars in the yard of the yellow house and strange people inside it — sad people, pacing slowly, in a daze, like people do when they stumble out of a wrecked car, having seen death up close but walking away from it. They were whispering sad things that my ears could hardly make out but my sorrow filled in. I looked around, and through a gap among the unfamiliar folks I saw Big Mama slumped in a chair, face swollen, jaw drooped, eyes blood red and holding the last puddles of a flood of tears. This was bad.

James ran to Jed's room, the last place he had seen him, but Jed wasn't there. He wasn't anywhere. He was gone. Dead, they told us, their manner grave, doing their best to choke back their own sadness and lessen ours.

Nothing could have prepared me. The earth shook. I was now old enough to know what death meant, what it really meant to lose someone you loved, not just people sleeping in a big ol' suitcase, but the hollow-making finality of it all. Overcome, I stood still and cried. I didn't know what to do. I didn't know how to hold my body. I closed my eyes because I didn't want to look into Big Mama's.

I couldn't believe it. I went to the bedroom so that I could see for myself. The room was cleaner than I had ever seen it. The bed was perfectly made, without a wrinkle. But Jed wasn't there. Life was gone from that room. Big Mama would never sleep in that room again.

I wandered around the house, lost and shell-shocked. I overheard Big Mama talking to someone on the phone. "He jus' start coughin', coughin' up a lots of blood, and dat was it."

And that was it. My first father, the one who knew what love was, gone. The ocean had dried up. And that changed Big Mama in ways that I was unable and unwilling to handle.

She hung a plaque with the Serenity Prayer on it next to the front door:

> God, grant me the serenity to accept
>   the things I cannot change,
> Courage to change the things I can,
> And wisdom to know the difference.

But serenity was now the furthest thing from that little yellow house.

Jed had held Big Mama's heart and seemed to take half of it with him when he crossed over. His death scarred her deeply. Most of the ache she kept in, but some leaked out.

She began to spank us kids more frequently and more severely. Sometimes she used a switch. Other times she used one of Jed's old belts. Once I saw her beat James with a water hose.

This was an odd and unsettling turn for me.

My mother was not cut from this cloth. As unforgiving as she could be when crossed by grown folks, my mother didn't take well to the notion of spanking children. She spanked, but rarely. Maybe it was a generational easing. Maybe it was her unending rebellion against Big Mama.

My mother told us that Big Mama had a mean streak, but I had never known it. My mother often recounted a story of a particularly harsh beating she had received. Big Mama had assumed that my mother had done something wrong. When my mother tried to explain, Big Mama told her to shut up and started whipping her. Refusing to be silenced, my mother kept yelling, "Mama, let me tell ya! Mama, let me tell ya!" Infuriated by my mother's insolence, Big Mama kept beating her. Eventually, Grandpa Bill had to step in and tell Big Mama, "Don't beat ha no mo'!" Neither one of them was going to give up anytime soon, or ever after.

Even when my mother thought it necessary to spank us she couldn't always bring herself to do it.

Like the time at the hairdresser's. Twice a month we boys would go there with my mother. The hairdresser lived in a rundown house at the end of a dead-end road, past a small sugarcane farm with a one-mule press. She had transformed her modest living room, crowded with knickknacks and covered in family pictures, into a makeshift salon. A beautician's chair sat in the middle of the room, where she used flame-heated irons to fry my mother's hair into neat rows of tight curls, small clouds of sulfur-scented smoke rising from each ringlet.

There was a lumpy, threadbare sofa facing the chair, and another one in a small alcove off to the right, where we boys sat with the hairdresser's mother, who never spoke but always chewed gum, amazingly producing several popped bubbles with every chomp.

We sometimes had to wait there for hours, under strict orders from our mother not to cause a commotion or ask for, or accept, any food or drink — it would have been rude.

"You better not go nowhere and act like I ain't never fed you."

One day at the hairdresser's Robert got really thirsty but was afraid to ask for water. Suddenly he sprang to his feet, eyes closed, arms outstretched, with limp wrists like the mummies in the television cartoons, and began to walk slowly, taking goose steps, while dragging out his words: "I . . . want . . . some . . . wa-ter. Give . . . me . . . some . . . wa-ter." My mother sat straight up in the chair, head half done, fuming. The other women, waiting their turn in the chair, laughed hysterically, urging on my brother's performance. "He sleepwalkin', gurl! Don't wake 'im up! They say it's dang'ous when you wake 'em up."

We thought that surely this little act, though hilarious, would get Robert beaten. When we got in the car, my mother chastised him while she fought a smile — "I shoulda to'e yo' behind up" — but she never spanked him. It was just too funny.

Big Mama didn't seem to have that lighter side anymore. It seemed to have left with Jed from the room containing the bed that now had no wrinkles. She seemed given to pain and sorrow without him. Ironically, in Big Mama's job as a housekeeper and babysitter, she was the most gentle, even-tempered, quick-to-laugh person you could imagine — the grandmother I wished I could have back. Maybe this was just a survival skill — though I doubt it, based on the number of wallet-sized pictures of white children tucked into the corners of the frames that held our portraits. I could never reconcile those two sides of her.

I would still go to Kiblah to stay for a couple of weeks in the summers, but things had changed too much and the good feelings were fading. It was no longer the safe, beautiful place it once had been.

. . .

That fall I was six years old, on the edge of my seat, clinging to the dashboard of a speeding car. My mother was behind the wheel, cradling her pistol, trying to catch a woman we had never met.

It was Thanksgiving Day, and just hours earlier our home had been filled with the sounds of excitement and the smell of food. Grandpa Bill had come from Houston. He was newly separated from his beautiful young wife. Big Mama had come from Arkansas, newly widowed by Jed. My father was there as well, newly exiled from my mother's affections.

It was a year that had torn at the fabric of our family, yet there we were, all together, smiling and laughing, resetting our faith, and reaffirming our love.

The air was filled with the smell of celebration — fruit and nuts, cakes and pies, ham and turkey, cornbread dressing and giblet gravy.

As always, Grandpa Bill held forth with his stories. He talked and laughed loudly like a man trying to be heard across a field, happy that the day's work was done. No one could tell a story like him, the way he locked eyes on you and drew you in. He started slowly, setting the scene with colorful details. Then his voice would begin to swell and his tempo quicken. By the time he reached the climax, he was screaming the words and howling with laughter, as were we.

Between his stories, he'd offer his opinion of me and my brothers. Like my father, he was impressed with my brothers' resourcefulness and break-it-down-and-fix-it-up nature. But he didn't know what to make of me, a boy who clung so closely to his mother. He would often say, as if I wasn't there, "That boy is never going to leave Billie's side." He said it not out of malice, but it hurt every time all the same. I knew even then that it meant he thought I would never make much of myself, that I would be stuck under her wing, afraid to spread my own.

I didn't agree with his assessment, but I didn't know how to refute it. All I knew was that I was smarter than I was strong. And that I was drawing something special from my mother. I was learning more by following her and watching her than anyone had ever set out to teach me. I just had no idea if it would be enough to help me make it in the world without her.

That Thanksgiving, Big Mama chatted Grandpa Bill up and egged him on. She openly flirted with him. He gently brushed her aside. It was easy to see what had drawn them to each other and what had made their union unsustainable. They amplified each other, but to a dangerous degree. There were no brakes. Neither of them had the will or the power to turn it off, only to turn it up. Besides, the fact that Big Mama was nearly his age made her too old for his current tastes. But that didn't stop the old girl from trying.

My mother bounced about in the kitchen, clinking pots, occasionally yelling a playful interjection or letting loose a belly laugh. While Big Mama's presence often irritated my mother, Grandpa Bill's presence excited her. He was the parent in whom she delighted. She was his namesake. She lit up for him, vying for his attention, bending over backward to make sure that he was comfortable and satisfied, still trying desperately to be daddy's little girl.

My father sat quietly, occasionally managing a grin or a chuckle, but mostly trying to blend into the background of a family to which he no longer belonged. My mother continued allowing him to visit, particularly on the holidays, for the sake of me and my brothers.

Soon my mother called everyone to the table, my grandfather said a prayer, and we dug in. That was what I loved about Thanksgiving: it was one of the only times that we ate together at the table. Most of the time we ate on the run or in our rooms with plates in our laps.

After dinner, we lounged around, drifting in and out of conversation and in and out of consciousness as my mother and Big Mama put away food and washed dishes. The phone rang. My mother answered it, but there was no response on the other end. After a few seconds, the caller hung up. My mother thought nothing of it. A few minutes later, the same thing — a ring, an answer, but no response. This kept up for more than an hour. My mother grew suspicious and irritated.

Then, on one of her trips from the kitchen to the dining room, she caught sight of a car creeping by outside. The joy drained from her face. Her eyes widened and her lips pursed. It was the car of one of my father's women — had to be. That was who had been playing on the phone, hoping that eventually he, not my mother, would answer. Now she had shown up. It was an act of disrespect, and disrespect was my mother's trigger.

Without saying a word, she walked out of the door and got into her car. As usual, I followed, ever the mama's boy. We quickly looped around the block until we caught sight of the woman's car again. Now my mother was sure. Her outrage boiled over. The woman had practically come to our front door. She had violated my mother's zone of dignity. Now she would see how much of a mistake that had been.

When we got all the way around the block, my mother stopped in front of our house and gave me instructions: "Go in there and get my pistol outta my pockabook and don't let nobody see you." She wanted to keep her eye on the woman's car. She was so blinded by rage that she couldn't see how wrong it was to send a six-year-old child to retrieve a loaded gun.

My mother wasn't a troublemaker, but if trouble came calling, it would be met with force. That happy Thanksgiving Day — in her mind, pumped up by hours of Grandpa Bill's stories about gun-pulling and chain-whipping — trouble had come calling. That was what Grandpa Bill did to folks, what must have made him such a great soldier: he made everyone around him feel braver, more reckless, more the defenders of honor than they had been before.

I walked into the house, got the gun, tucked it into my pants, covered it with my shirt, and walked back out to the waiting car. No one suspected a thing. I got in and passed my mother the gun, and we sped off. We soon caught up to the woman, but when she realized we were chasing her, she pushed the pedal to the metal. My mother responded in kind. We raced through the town's narrow streets, then onto Interstate 20. The woman was weaving through cars, dodging onto the shoulder, and dipping into the median. My mother was right behind her, not giving an inch. I clung to the dashboard, adrenaline pulsing through my body. I was excited and terrified at the same time, repeating in my mind, "Git ha, Mama! Git ha!"

I don't know what made my mother stop chasing the woman, but I always believed that at least in part it was the image of her little boy awash in her bloodlust, glassy-eyed and salivating for a horrible end to the chase. It was sad and wrong, and she knew it. It was dangerous and futile, and she knew it. So she took her foot off the gas pedal and let it all go. Her indignation was costing her her sanity. The car, and my heartbeat, began to slow. The woman got away and my mother gave up — gave up fighting my father's women and her ghosts. She set herself free.

There is nothing like the presence of a gun, and an earnest intent to use it, to draw the totality of a life into sharp relief. That was a lesson I would learn early and often. But even more important was the idea that, at any moment, we all had the awesome and underutilized power to simply let go of our past and step beyond it.

We went back home and rejoined the conversation as if nothing had happened.

Later, my mother made plates of the leftovers and delivered them to people in the community who needed a good meal and a little help. That was the way it was with my mother, constantly vacillating between hotheaded vigilante and beneficent exemplar — between the temper she had inherited from Grandpa Bill and the temperance she had absorbed from Mam' Grace.

Also that afternoon, Grandpa Bill, an avid gun collector, drove me and my brothers to an open spot in the woods and let us take turns firing his .45-caliber pistol. He didn't know that I'd had enough gunplay for one day.

When it was my turn, I pulled the trigger and the weapon exploded in my hand, jolting my body, the clap leaving me momentarily deaf and securing in me the profound discomfort of how easily and irreversibly its lethal power could be unleashed.

Once that bullet left the chamber there was nothing you could do to bring it back. Once you shot at someone, everything else was up to God. A mistake seemed too easy to make. Something done in a fit anger or after a few swigs of alcohol — the way I had seen and heard of guns being used — could last forever.

I thought to myself that, unlike my grandfather and my mother, I could never shoot at another person. That feeling wouldn't last always.

3

Chester

Summers in north Louisiana in some ways were brutal. The heat was heavy. It pushed back against anything that tried to speed up. The sun cracked the earth, chasing everything that could escape into the shade, sucking the life from everything that couldn't, like the fried earthworms that littered the streets, the ones that tried to slither across during the cool of the morning but didn't make it before the sun heated the asphalt like a griddle.

The thick air was a swarming mass of horseflies and houseflies, moths and mosquitoes, wasps, yellow jackets, and bumblebees. Folks sat around smoky fires fanning rags to ward off the bugs and to stay free of stings. To keep the snakes out of the grass we sprinkled lime along the fencerows, which was supposed to burn their bellies as they crossed them. It never seemed to work.

In other ways, the summers were beautiful and sweet. There were magnolia blossoms up high and jonquil flowers down low. Honeysuckle-scented breezes wafted through the long days. Fruit and nuts ripened in the trees that cast cool shade. Clouds of pollen filled the air like flurries of snow.

Even more than in the winter, our house in the summer played host to a steady stream of kinfolk and old folk, friends and freeloaders — sitting for a spell, getting a hot plate and a cool glass, sharing tall tales and deep laughs. Sometimes we got a visit from my mother's great-uncle, who was both Mam' Grace's half-brother and her first cousin, since their mothers were sisters and had children by the same man. Uncle Solomon was a deacon in his church and an open polygamist who lived with his three "wives," only one of whom was his legal bride. He maintained a separate house for the only "wife" who bore him children. The women plotted and schemed about how and when they would leave him, but they never did.

At other times we were visited by another uncle and aunt to whom we were also twice related — he was my mother's uncle and she was my father's aunt. Aunt Edna was a pillow-soft woman with extremely fair skin that was jiggly and cold to the touch, dripping like wax from her frame. Kinfolk accused her of masking her chronic laziness with make-believe illnesses. Her body started to atrophy from lack of use, and the illnesses folks accused her of manufacturing eventually manifested. The old lady who had cried wolf was looking the wolf in the face. Her husband was a dark, whip-thin man, with teeth as white as bone china and a habit of talking faster than we could listen. He was an army veteran and retained some of the military rigor in his posture and demeanor, and also in his a sense of duty, expressed in his catering to his wife's endless stream of dictates.

Sometimes a cousin would spend a couple of weeks with us. This summer, our cousin Chester came to stay for a spell. Chester was the son of my mother's brother Henry, who as a boy had followed Big Mama to Arkansas when my mother had stayed behind. Uncle Henry was a man who defied easy definition because he seemed to exist outside the rules.

· · ·

Uncle Henry had been a good-looking young man, cavalier and quix-
otic. He had gone to Grambling College — twenty miles west of Gibsland — on a band scholarship, but soon joined the army, where folks
said he began to make good. While stationed overseas he got caught
doing something bad — something to do with military secrets, as best
I could tell from the fragments I heard whispered by shamefaced kinfolk. Whatever it was, Grandpa Bill's Silver Star was tarnished by the
foolish acts of his son, who was sent to the military prison in Leavenworth, Kansas.

Uncle Henry fell so spectacularly that he no longer seemed to want
to get back up, or to care what people said about him being down.
The only time I remembered seeing him was at the funerals of Mam'
Grace and Papa Joe, when the prison had granted him leave to attend.
To me, during those brief visits, even though his physical appearance
was a bit wild and wayworn, there seemed a certain freedom in his failure — a liberation from the concerns of the world, which I found fascinating.

He emerged from prison a changed man — a drinking, carousing Casanova who mined the juke joints for easy pleasures, repeating
the old saw "They all look good at closing time." He apparently didn't
always look particularly closely at closing time. He once picked up a
woman who wasn't a woman. He didn't discover her deception until
they were rolling around doing the things that people do when they
leave juke joints.

"When I flipped that gal ova, she had a thang big'n mine."

"What did you do, Uncle Henry?" my brothers asked, giggling.

"Well, hell, I was almost finished then!"

The family laughed it off as a mistake easily made when liquor dulls
the senses.

Uncle Henry constantly cycled through women — moving in, making babies, and moving on. I understood even then there was something about him — in his smile, in the way he walked, in the way he
sweet-mouthed folks — that appealed to a blind and boundless faith in

some women that their love alone would be sufficient to lift fallen men or fix broken ones.

"Slick as owl shit," my mother said of him.

Chester had Uncle Henry's impish smile, full of subtlety and mischief, the kind that could be used as a tool, a shield, and a weapon, the kind that made people believe things they shouldn't.

He had stayed with us before, but this time was different. Almost from the moment he arrived, he made clear that he was interested in playing with me more than with my older brothers, who were closer to his age. I was so starved for attention — my own brothers rarely seemed to want to play with me — that this surprised and delighted me. Nathan even gave up his spot in our bed and slept on the sofa so that Chester and I could sleep together. Chester and I laughed and played all day and all night. I was only seven, but now I felt like a big boy.

One afternoon, Chester persuaded me to steal candy from the store up the street.

Next door to our house, past the fencerow where wildflowers and blackberries grew and past a field of majestic sunflowers, lived Mrs. Bertha, a joyless, licorice-colored woman who kept her curls shaped under a black hairnet. She ran a one-room, cinderblock store crowded close to the house she shared with her mixed-race husband. The store had a cement floor with paths worn glass-smooth from people walking the same routes over many years. It had poor lighting and sparse furnishings. Just inside the door, on the left, was a homemade, glass-paned case stocked with stale candies — Tootsie Rolls, Red Hots, caramel squares, SweeTarts, and Lemonheads, my favorite. To the right was an intermittently stocked soda machine that dispensed ice-cold, bottled drinks — root beer, orange, and grape. In the middle of the room was an old wooden desk on which sat a broken cash register and two large glass jars, one containing sugar cookies, the other dill pickles.

Beyond the desk was an old stove and a couple of tables where Mrs. Bertha served lunch and dinner to bedraggled old men who no longer had — or never had — the luxury of an able wife. They were men who wore their loneliness in their clothes. There was no one to soak the stains and scrub them out before they set, no one to mend the holes and bite the thread when the job was done.

I reluctantly agreed to steal from the store. I didn't realize that this was a test of my willingness to break the rules and of my ability to keep it secret. I didn't realize that Chester wanted me to make my bones by killing that part of me that was still innocent.

We entered, went behind the case, and chose our loot. I fidgeted. My eyes darted. I was a panicky mass of anxiety. We went to the counter and paid for the candy in our hands, not the candy in our pockets. On the way home, Chester celebrated like he had just won a game. I was overcome by guilt.

I thought about what I'd done, and I did not approve. I decided to return the candy, hoping that doing so would be seen as honorable, and that Mrs. Bertha wouldn't tell my mother. I returned to the store alone. As I stammered through my apology and slid the candies across the desk, Mrs. Bertha sat silent, angry, and brewing with judgment. Before I got home, she had called my mother and told her what I had done. My mother was disappointed.

That evening I hurried off to bed, retreating from my own reproof, hoping to put that day behind me.

But the shame of stealing candy would pale in comparison to what came next.

Sometime during the night, I was awoken by the feeling of something happening to me below my waist. My underwear was pushed down around my thighs. Chester was pushed up behind me, holding me, the most private part of him moving against me. My body snapped straight and stiff like a cedar fencepost — an instant, reflexive resistance. I jerked, trying to move away, but he held me tighter. I didn't know what was going on or what to do.

I couldn't get away. I recalled my mother's silent submission to my father. Maybe if I just lay hushed and still, I too would rise in the morning moving happily about. But this just felt different, and wrong.

I tried to think it through, to find the words that would make him stop. Those words never came. The words that did come were like a thousand sparks in the darkness — too random to make sense, too fleeting to shed light.

And his words rang in my head, whispered in pulses of hot breath from wet lips moving slowly, so close to my ear that they occasionally touched.

"Relax, it's just a game. Relax, it's just a game." He repeated the line over and over, dripping the words into my mind, murmuring soft and metered in a tone usually reserved for the calming of a colicky baby, a carnal incantation meant to loosen my limbs and shield his sins.

I seemed to float above the illicit scene, in it, but not.

His body never entered mine, but to me, in that moment, that seemed a distinction without a difference. In that moment, I reached the fraying point between my spirit and my body — in that moment, the connection between them was irreparably severed.

Soon his grip loosened, and he pushed back and propped himself up on one elbow, still facing in my direction. I rolled onto my back and stared up toward the ceiling at the spot where I had imagined my spirit floating. He said, "It's just a game. Look, scoot up behind me." He rolled over on his other side so that he was now facing away from me and toward the wall. I lay there stunned, unable to think or act. "Scoot up!" he barked, looking back over his shoulder. I turned and scooted up behind him, unclear of what I was doing or why. "See, now turn over." He rolled back over until he was again facing me, then rolled me over so that my back was once again facing him, and he moved up behind me again.

In the same room where Mam' Grace had turned and released her life and sent everyone screaming, I had been turned and mine taken without so much as a peep. Dead all the same. Just different.

Eventually, Chester tired and went to sleep. I lay there on my side, shocked and silent. I stared at the dim light shining through the crack beneath the door, thinking that Nathan lay just beyond it, thinking that had I screamed, he would have come running. But what would I have told him? Surely I would have gotten in trouble. Somehow this was my fault. Surely I had done something awful to make Chester do what he had done. I just couldn't figure out what it was. Or maybe there was another reason, one I thought worse. Maybe I had been curious and willing. Maybe I had wanted him to do what he had done and that's why I hadn't screamed. That possibility to me was even more frightening than the first.

But, either way, it was obviously me.

The day after Chester locked his arms around me and pushed up behind me, I sat hiding and grieving on the stubbled ground inside a maze that one of my brothers had mowed in the tall grass of the field where Papa Joe had raised hogs. Chester walked by on the street and noticed me there. He came into the maze and knelt beside me. "Hey, let's do what we did last night again today."

This time, the words came, haltingly, "No, I don't want to."

He said nothing, but his cheeks dropped, and the impish smile fell flat before twisting itself into a scowl. He was not pleased. He surveyed my face for a moment as I stared at the ground, trying to avoid the wither of his gaze, looking down at the cut grass wilting in the heat. Then he got up and left me there and never played with me or spoke a kind word to me ever again.

I don't know how to describe the sound of a world crashing. Maybe there is no sound, just a great emptiness, an enveloping sorrow, a creeping nothingness that coils itself around you like a stiff wire. I wanted to scream, but couldn't — wanted to cry, but couldn't. I was dead now, and dead boys forget how to cry.

Confused and hurt and irrational, I did the worst thing: I deflected blame from the person who'd hurt me most to the person who loved me most. Why had my mother let Chester sleep with me? Why couldn't she see what he had done? What I couldn't muster the courage to let cross my lips was engraved on my face. I was crestfallen, morose — the cold shadow of a child consumed. Why couldn't she see it?

Part of me wanted desperately to tell her, but another part of me believed that was beyond the realm of possibility — she would punish me, or kill him, or both.

On the one hand, I wanted her to know without hearing, to see something that I couldn't say. But she couldn't. She couldn't see it. She couldn't read my mind as I had been sure she could. On the other hand, I knew how much she worked and worried. I knew how hard it was for us to grow the vegetables and raise the hogs. This thing that had happened to me was only a few minutes in the middle of a summer night — big to me, but small in the grand sweep of things.

Then I had the idea that it wasn't her that I needed in that moment so much as a father. This was an issue among boys and men. I needed a man who could understand and help me make sense of what happened, a heavy arm in whose crook I could hide. I needed a father like Jed, someone with the kind of eyes that forgave secret shame before it scarred the throat in the speaking. But I had no father. Jed was dead. And my real father, who had hardly ever been a real father, was lost to me.

There was no one to break my fall. There was no one to save me.

I had never thought it possible that a boy could be drawn to another the way Chester had been drawn to me, but now the idea was woven through the fiber of me — once broken, forever altered. The idea wouldn't exist in me as an attraction to boys' bodies, or even to a boy in particular, but — the way it had been introduced to me — as the pull of attention, the idea of being chosen. I hadn't seen Chester's body that night. It had been shrouded in darkness. It was in my mind that I believed the thing had happened, and it was in my mind that I now fused together abuse and attraction. It was the embrace — the thing that I no longer got in this house of busy people and in this neighborhood where no one called me Char'es Baby — that I thought had held me quiet.

Chester's betrayal left me gun-shy around aggressive boys. They could no longer be trusted. I had so misjudged Chester's intent, that look he gave, that I would spend the rest of my life studying people's faces, trying to pick up on the hints of kindness and the residue of ill intent, those subtle cues that separate friend from foe. Until I could interpret those clues, I retreated — from conversation, from family, and from friends — for my own survival.

As I retreated, he followed, with an endless tirade of putdowns designed to keep me from telling and to undermine my credibility if I did.

"You a punk."

"Everybody say you a punk."

"Punk" was the word young people used to describe boys suspected of liking other boys. Old people said "sissy." No one said "gay." "Punk" was the kind of word that people spat out rather than spoke, with a mix of pity, shame, and disgust. "Punk!" with lips curled up like the tongue needed scraping.

I wasn't sure if what Chester said was true or not. I did know that punk was the worst thing that you could call a boy. The world around me made it clear: punks were a waste of a boy, an offense to God, and a violation of nature. And I knew that my new refusal to hang with other boys gave his accusations more credence.

On and on it went, every time I saw him. I grew exhausted, having been unprepared for such a lasting, targeted assault. My psyche was being rubbed raw. The fact that my brothers were often witnesses to his taunting and either nonchalantly ignored it or passively encouraged it was something I never forgot or forgave. I could see what they were doing. I could see why they chuckled when Chester laid into me: they were making distance between us, making sure that the stigma settling over me didn't cast a shadow on them.

Chester's strategy worked — I never told. I thought that if I suppressed what he had done, I could forget it, suffocate it, make it disappear. Instead, the secret fed on my silence, morphing it into something more dangerous. It spread, consuming me, eating me hollow. In the fall, we went back to school, and I began to disappear.

Since first grade, I had not gone to school in Gibsland, where we lived, but in Ringgold, where my mother taught home economics. William was no longer able to take Robert and me to school on the bicycle because he had moved up to the high school, so Robert and I began going with my mother to Ringgold. But Robert quickly tired of the commute, so she allowed him to transfer back to Gibsland Elementary. She thought him old enough to catch the bus to school in Gibsland on his own. But not me.

The good part about going alone to school with my mother was that I got to spend more time with her, time that I didn't have to share with my brothers. The bad part was that it made full friendships with other children difficult. I didn't see my Gibsland friends in school or my Ringgold friends at home.

The only friend I had both during school and after was the son of another teacher, but that friendship would end sadly. His mother and mine became friends and often had after-school duty on the same days, which made it easy for the two of us boys to play together. But soon after we became friends he was diagnosed with a brain tumor. The doctors tried to remove the growth, but they were unable to get it all. So they had to operate again. And again. With each operation, more and more of my friend was taken away, until he was completely gone.

One of the only times I remember feeling alive the year after Chester's betrayal was the night of the school pageant.

Ringgold's school had been integrated, but in some ways it continued to support segregation. Every year the school held a pageant to crown a king and queen of each of the three divisions of the school. Actually, two pageants were held simultaneously, on the same night, on the same stage — one for whites, one for blacks. The year after Chester's betrayal, I was in the pageant.

I was just going through the motions until an escort took us one by one into a classroom to be interviewed by the judges. It was the first time I realized I could read people's faces and become the person they wished to see. The judges wanted three parts charm and one part mischief, a kind of controlled precociousness, so I turned it on, and they lit up.

It wasn't real, but I could make them believe that it was. I could graft life onto my dead self. I knew immediately that there was power in that ability. That's what happens with boys like me: they get good at creating and pretending. It's how they survive.

That night I won as king of the black children's elementary school division. They gave me a crown and a scepter and a little golden trophy inscribed with the title "Little Master," the black one. This turned out not to be all good, though, because I ran afoul of the school bully, who thought himself handsome and cheated of the win. So now I had a bully in my family and a bully in school.

But for the rest of the school year I was gone, there in body but not in spirit, drifting deeper into darkness. My work suffered, and the teachers moved me to the slow class because they thought me unable to handle the regular one. My mother protested. Most of the time, no matter how well or poorly her children performed, my mother didn't make much of it. She exerted only enough pressure to keep us from completely slipping, like the pinch of a clothespin. But this was a step too far. She didn't know what was wrong with me, but she knew that I wasn't slow.

I was moved back to the regular class, but I would never again be a regular boy.

That was the year I came to believe that my young life was no longer worth living, that ending it was not only possible but preferable, that I should fully commit my body to the fate that my mind had already assigned it. I was eight years old.

One night someone volunteered to take my brothers and me to

the roller-skating rink in Minden. I had a pounding headache, but still I wanted to go. After all, a trip to the rink was rare. I grabbed a bottle of aspirin, tucked it into my pocket with my junkyard talismans, and crawled into the car.

Inside the rink, the skaters propelled themselves with synchronized lunges, dipping and swaying to the rhythm of disco tracks blaring from giant speakers. They lapped the rink in unison, like a dog chasing its tail and with the same simple-minded delirium — laughing and dancing. Lovers held hands. Learners held on.

Hundreds of tiny wheels clacked and whizzed, the sound coalescing into a single buzz, and thousands of tiny dots, reflected from a dangling disco ball, sprayed the room with whimsy.

I left the floor to take some aspirin, and as I looked out on the scene from the railing, all the world went quiet — the only remaining sound was the thump of my heartbeat in my temples. I was having fun, but now even in the happiest of times, sorrow lurked just below the surface.

I felt my spirit again begin to cleave from my body. I seemed to be watching from beyond my body, and in this place the weariness of pushing back against a wall of sadness melted away. For a moment, I was free again.

And that was the thing. I felt free only when I could separate myself from myself, when I could imagine that I was distinct from my body and life. There in the ethereal nothingness, in the quiet space of my mind, I found peace.

I liked it there and didn't want to leave. I didn't want to return to the world. Life was too hard and treacherous. I was too weak and vulnerable. I couldn't live in sorrow forever. So, in that instance, with no forethought, I decided that night would be my last.

I had never thought of suicide before and had never remembered speaking the word, but in a flash the thought fell on me so completely and so agreeably, it was as if I'd planned it.

I dug the bottle of aspirin from my pocket. I was going to take them all. I had no idea if they would kill me, but I hoped they would. But then the questions came: Would it hurt? How long would it take? Would my mother be sad? Would I go to hell for committing suicide? Heavy questions piling up like boots by a door.

Before I could form answers, one of my mother's songs came to save me, one of the songs she sang when we were alone in the car on our drives to and from Ringgold, when I was drifting off to sleep or pretending to, staring out the window, catching fleeting glimpses of green-hooded mallards and white-tailed deer. She often said that she wished she were able to sing, and was disappointed when she realized that she lacked the gift. So she rarely sang.

But there in the car, out of earshot of everyone except me, she sang. She sang about run-around men and hold-tight women, about sticky-sweet love and salty-dry longing, about rest waiting up in the next life and the weight pressing down on this one — songs like the gospel standard "Please Be Patient with Me," Mel and Tim's blues classic "Starting All Over Again," and Betty Wright's R&B hit "Clean Up Woman." They were the kinds of songs that dug down until they hit something soft and raw. They set the story of her life to a melody, and she sang them from an honest place with little regard for talent or judgment. With these songs she tapped into a more tender part of herself, one I rarely saw, one where she didn't have to be stoic and phlegmatic, where she could release the tension that drew back her shoulders and acknowledge the desire that tickled her flesh, where she could accept the idea of frailty and entertain the possibility of tears. It was a place where she could just be beautifully human — Billie in the whole.

That was the gift.

And so there it was, not summoned and without warning, pushing its way through the crowd of questions, "Take My Hand, Precious Lord," one of the songs my mother sang hard and true out of her heart and into a steering wheel, coming to save me.

Precious Lord, take my hand
Lead me on, let me stand
I'm tired, I'm weak, I'm lone.
Through the storm, through the night
Lead me on to the light
Take my hand, precious Lord, lead me home.

I didn't know why that song, of all things, came into my head, but I took it as a sign. I believed that God was trying to tell me something: that He would somehow make a way for me to survive, that I had to be brave and patient, that this was not my last night.

I swallowed two aspirin, flung myself back out onto the hardwood to the sound of Earth, Wind and Fire's "Shining Star," and never thought about suicide again.

I decided that night that I would turn to God. Surely He could fix things.

My family wasn't extremely religious, but we were observant and reverent. Every second and fourth Sunday, the preacher we shared with another church came to preach at ours. We sometimes went to church on those Sundays. Our church was Shiloh Baptist. It was my mother's home church, located in Sparta, the now-defunct town that was once the parish seat, some twenty miles southeast of Gibsland and not far from Bienville, where my father now lived. The remaining community was now called Shiloh, after the church.

To get there we drove south, between two sweet potato farms set atop a hill, facing each other. They sold most of the roots wholesale, but we bought them retail, for pies, soufflés, chips, and candying. The farm on the west side of the road had a caged monkey at the entrance. I liked that farm. I would stare at the monkey, in awe of how familiar it looked, and yet how foreign it was. I thought about how much I would like to see it outside of its cage, but I was glad that it wasn't.

Farther on, we passed over rolling, forested hills. My mother often reminded us that Papa Joe's father had owned one of those hills, but white folks had found a way to take it from him. She said that another great-grandfather had also owned hundreds of acres in the area, and his property, too, had been taken from him by white folks.

The sad irony of it all was that some of those hills were now dotted with oil rigs and others covered in farmed trees, reaping wealth for their owners, and we had to drive through them on our way to church so that we could pray that we would have enough to eat and make do.

Soon we were pulling into the church parking lot. Shiloh Baptist stood at a fork in the road. It was a humble, wood-framed building elevated on brick pedestals, and the earth had settled and shifted beneath it in a way that left the church slightly warped.

It was a bit tattered, but exactly right: an imperfect outside made perfect by virtue of what was happening inside. It was the kind of building that remembered things, deep-down things, things that rode tears into the world, telling them back to anyone old enough or wise enough to know how to listen with their eyes.

Ushers with taut faces and white gloves held the doors like angels at heaven's gate, directing us at the proper time — and only then — to an open pew, the ends of which had been polished to a shine by generations of hands using them for support.

The deacon board was arrayed to the right of the simple wooden pulpit, and the mother board was to the left. These places were reserved for the church elders — men with flour-sack bellies lapping straining belts, women with chestnut-colored stockings rolling down pecan-colored shins — most well past their allotted three score and ten. They were our counsels and conscience, having seen the world in all its majesty and cruelty.

The creaky center aisle was where bodies moved forward to be transformed. It's where fathers gave away young brides, where caskets gave cover for the dead, and where sinners gave over weary souls.

Women in long dresses and big hats waved paper fans that looked like a rabble of butterflies set down on a patch of flowers. Little boys scratched at itchy suits. Little girls dug hard candy from their mothers' purses. A small table rested in front of the pulpit, where members handed over their meager offerings and the deacons opened the service with prayer and song.

The deacons shouted those songs and sang the prayers, all with the cadence and volume of field workers — kneeling on one knee, eyes closed, heads bowing, swaying, craning, punctuating the words as they erupted from their bodies.

The song was always the same:

> Guide me, O thou great Jehovah!
> Pilgrim through this barren land!

The congregation trailed with the same verse, only in a protracted fusion of singing and moaning, dripping slow and thick like syrup.

The sound vibrated in the mouth and stirred the soul. It was a purging — burdens flowing out of us and into Him. The song proclaimed that the time had come for all who heard it to be still so that the spirit could move.

This was a time before men wore crayon-colored suits, when choirs focused more on dirges than dancing, and sermons were more about piety than earthly increase.

Our pastor, Reverend Brown, was a decent man with a good reputation. Not every congregation was so lucky. Preaching was a profession dotted with the supposedly repentant who touted their checkered pasts as a testimony to God's grace — "Ef He can save a wratch like me . . . Hallelujah! Thank ya, JEE-suss!"

I, for one, was fascinated by Reverend Brown and his sermons, the way he played on opposites — reward and punishment, angels and demons, a gentle Savior and a vengeful God — flipping back and forth like a cook using a two-page recipe.

At our church, we came late and left early because my mother tired easily of the prolonged orchestration of it all. For her, anything over an hour was too long. "It don't take the Lord two hours to save *nobody*," she'd say. We would wait for the ushers to call us forward for the offering, and instead of returning to our seats afterward, we'd break for the door. She dared not leave in the middle of the sermon, lest God take it as disrespect. She reminded us of the story that Mam' Grace told her about a man who had cursed at a preacher and thrown a Bible. "He shook till the day he died!"

When we got home from church, my mother opened the windows and cleaned the house to done-me-wrong, baby-come-back, ghetto-love anthems from her small collection of scratched records — Marvin Gaye, Gladys Knight, Al Green, Otis Redding, and Johnnie Taylor. This Sunday morning-to-afternoon musical switch would reflect the framework of my faith — an ever-swirling mix of the orthodox and the secular.

Although religion, with all its talk of dying and blood and burning, scared me, I was fascinated by God's use of fouled-up men and fallen women to extend His message; by His liberation of the poor, the outcast, and the infirm; and by His obsession with improbable transformations and inappropriate ascensions. If ever a body needed a savior, I did.

In the fall after Chester's betrayal, I walked the aisle to give myself over. But by then Shiloh wasn't the same Shiloh. The congregation had built itself a new building next door to the old one. It was a handsome brick church on a concrete slab, with crimson-upholstered pews and crimson-carpeted floors. It had a professional sound system, a beautifully lit, glassed-in baptismal pool, and an ornate pulpit. It had high vaulted ceilings and arches, wooden ribs with golden chandeliers hanging from their bosses. It was impressive but hollow — like a vanity. We no longer attended services in the building so full of life that it spoke to people's eyes, but in a building that sat cold and hushed.

The walk of redemption now felt more theatrical. Still, I was determined to make it. When Reverend Brown finished his sermon, he made his way around to the front of the pulpit, wiped sweat from his brow, and invited the unsaved to come forward.

"Won't sumbidy come dis moaning? Tamorr' MIGHT be too late!"

I rose from my seat to an outburst of clapping and an outpouring of amens and thank-you-Jesuses. My mother, surprised and proud, smiled at me as I made my way down the aisle, which that day seemed a mile long. When I reached Reverend Brown, he put his large hand on my small shoulder and turned me around to face the congregation.

"What's ya name, young man?"

"Charles McRay Blow," I said into the microphone he'd thrust in my face.

(When I was born, Nathan pleaded with my mother to name me Ray Charles, after the singer. Charles McRay was her compromise. She insisted we have the most traditional first names possible, to balance such an odd last one.)

"Do you believe that Jesus is the Son of God?" the preacher continued.

"Yes," I said, embarrassed and nervous.

"Do you believe that he died fa yo' sins?"

"Yes."

"Do you want to be baptized?"

I hesitated. Reverend Brown was big and burly and shined with the unctuous look of a man who'd just eaten half a ham. I was afraid of him. The times I'd seen him baptize someone, it had seemed to me a violent affair. And I couldn't swim. I didn't want to drown in church to keep from burning in hell.

"Well," I said, "I don't know 'bout *all that*."

The congregation burst into laughter as my mother slinked down in the pew. I made my way back to my seat. I was going to have to solve my problems on my own.

·   ·   ·

The Thursday before the first Sunday in August was Graveyard Working Day at the black cemetery in the historic hamlet of Mount Lebanon, three miles south of town, beyond the sweet potato farms. Mount Lebanon was an all-white community of folks who lived in a small cluster of well-maintained Greek Revival houses that hinted at a proud history. The community had been the center of wealth and scholarship in the region before the Civil War. It was the home of a university founded by an Irishman named Egan, brought to America by Thomas Jefferson. Folks said that Jefferson once called Egan "one of the ripest scholars of his age."

But during the Civil War the university gave over its buildings to army surgeons, who filled them with Confederate wounded. The school reopened after the war, but now it was gone, all remnants of it wiped clean from that place, folded into the forest.

The one surviving bit of glory was the Baptist church, said to be the oldest continuously operating Baptist church in the state, started by a mulatto preacher who built a balcony to seat the slaves apart from the white folks.

But segregation didn't end at the church doors; it extended into the cemetery.

Two burial grounds abutted each other — one for blacks, the other for whites. The black cemetery was filled with uneven rows of tiny, tilting gravestones. And those were the lucky folks. Some graves had no marker at all. Depending on how long ago it was dug, a grave was either just a rock-hard mound of dirt or a slight indentation from a casket that had long ago decayed and collapsed. In contrast, the white cemetery had a well-manicured, even lawn with gleaming monuments, perfectly aligned, reaching like giant arms toward heaven, each one seemingly taller than the last.

The two cemeteries were separated by a chainlink fence, lest anyone, living or dead, forget the rules — say, someone like the "white trash woman" who hung around the West End and had a baby by a black man. The way it was told to me, the baby died and the woman wanted to bury it with her family on the white side of the cemetery. When white folks found out that the baby was half black, they refused her, so she buried her baby on the black side as close to the fence as she could.

My mother told me that when she was a girl, every black family came on Graveyard Working Day and groomed their family's plot. It was like an all-day community picnic with the dead. A minister presided over the activities with a group prayer. People hoed weeds, raked leaves, cleared grass, and replaced sun-bleached plastic flowers. Elders recited family histories, connecting brief biographies and fascinating tales with each headstone as if flipping through the pages of a photo album.

But this year only a few families showed up. Overgrown graves and weed-covered plots were everywhere; it was not uncommon for a grave to get "lost." Our family brought only water and a few sandwiches and worked quickly and purposefully, leaving as soon as we could.

On a previous trip to the cemetery I'd learned that Chester had been a twin, but that his brother was stillborn. The dead baby had been buried in an unmarked grave in our family's area, somewhere to the left of Mam' Grace and Papa Joe, near the trunk of a large tree. But by the time I learned of Chester's twin, the grave had disappeared.

On this day I walked around that tree, looking for some evidence that the ground had once been turned — a slight indentation, the remains of a tiny mound, anything. I wanted to find that boy. My young mind couldn't help but imagine that he was dead because of Chester. How could Chester have lived and the other boy died? It was simple: Chester had killed him before they made it out into the world. He was another boy whose life Chester had taken. I figured that if I could find him, he could help me to survive, tell me some secret that he had learned too late to save himself.

I never found the grave. But, standing there under that tree, I imagined that Chester's twin could hear me, that we understood each other, and that there in that shaded spot we cried together.

His spirit was present there, as were the spirits of Papa Joe and

Mam' Grace. Like the boy's grave, I was lost too. But there, surrounded by them, I found the remnants of myself. There my soul could again be quiet, still and untroubled.

It was like the way I'd felt at the skating rink before I'd reached for the aspirin, except then it had felt more like surrendering to weakness. This felt more like gathering strength. In that moment in the graveyard I saw my own life and trials through the prism of past lives. In that moment the weight of my shame and separation was lifted.

There, among the sleeping souls of old folks and in the company of a dead boy, I came back to life. But a boy still walking can't stay in a graveyard, even a boy so recently broken and dead on the inside. I had to find a place to heal myself among the living.

4

The Punk Next Door

I spent much of my third-grade year hanging out with the punk next door.

At least that's what everyone called him. His real name was Shane. He was a year older than me and lived on the other side of the wooded lot into which my father had disappeared to escape my mother's gunshots.

If I was now two beats off in the dance that boys did to establish and affirm their masculinity and to find their place in the pack, Shane never even heard the music. But I didn't mind that about him. After all, I hadn't been touched by a punk. I'd been touched by a regular boy, a boy's boy. In fact, with Chester now calling me the same thing — punk — I secretly felt some kinship with Shane.

Still, I hated that word and didn't want the label to take hold with other folks because of my association with Shane. I wouldn't have been brave enough to walk into Shane's world if I had to do so alone. Luckily, another boy my age who'd just moved in down the street — a boy with no stigma other than newness — had also started to play at Shane's house. The new boy's presence gave cover for mine.

Everything about Shane said that he was different from other boys. He was not favored by nature. He had curves in places boys shouldn't have curves — hippy and chesty and none of it muscle, at least not in appearance. Even his face was different, the kind of face that held no tension in the brow or around the mouth. And his eyes were too soft and stretched too wide open, like they wanted to ask a question they didn't dare ask, a question that needed to be preceded by an apology.

As effete as Shane's manner was, there was a line he never crossed, as far as I knew, a line only ever crossed by two boys in town, both of whom had stopped pretending not to be punks, both of whom were my second cousins.

Both were starvation-thin. Both had wispy, processed hair grown long enough that it would move with a good snap of the neck. Both wore their pants high and their belts tight. And both walked with their wrists turned out — the kind of walk that tells the world that you prefer being chased to chasing.

They didn't even sit like other boys — gap-legged and sprawled out, taking up twice as much space as needed. Instead, they sat with knees together, hands pressed palm-to-palm, the way people do when praying, only their fingers weren't pointing up toward heaven but pushed down between their thighs. And they held their shoulders concave, bodies contracting, purposely making themselves smaller than they were, shrinking from the world. One had a lisp and the other hissed his *s*'s so high that they produced a faint whistle when they trailed off.

Lawrence was the cousin who whistled the *s*'s. His mother, my great-aunt Trudy, was a big-boned wig-splitter whom I once saw come to shoot a woman for sleeping with her husband. It was on a night when we still lived in the House with No Steps and our wringer washer had failed. My mother had taken our clothes to the laundromat, and, as always, she'd brought me with her. The only two people inside doing laundry were my mother and the cheating woman. I played outside, in and around the car.

Aunt Trudy whipped her car into the parking lot and jumped out, waving a pistol and yelling at the woman to come outside. My mother and the woman dropped to the floor. I rose up on the seat of our car to see what would happen. My mother yelled for me to get down; no one came outside. Soon Aunt Trudy got back in her car and drove away. She surely would have shot that woman if she'd been certain she wouldn't hit my mother and I wouldn't see.

Aunt Trudy wasn't a woman given to threats. She was the kind who bit first and barked later. Her idea of childhood stories was talking about the time she jumped from the bushes with a chain and beat a girl who told a lie. If you were on the side of right, you were good with Aunt Trudy. If you were on the side of wrong, God help you.

I often wondered how a boy as soft as Lawrence could come from such a tough woman. Maybe women like that sucked up so much of the strength in a house that not enough was left for all the men. Maybe that had happened to Lawrence. I worried that maybe it would happen to me.

Sometimes at night Lawrence would stop by the tiny upholstery shop kept by another cousin, down at the corner where our street met the highway. They were both related to my family, but not to each other. There Lawrence would talk slick and flirty and say things that he didn't dare say when the sun was up and staring eyes burned holes into him.

The shopkeeper was a Vietnam veteran who'd come back from the war with a metal plate in his head and something gone from it. He often worked late into the night, partly because he always seemed to be behind and partly because he never seemed to want to go home. He probably preferred his shop full of dead chairs to his house full of live people.

My brother Robert, the one who had walked like a mummy for the glass of water, was his apprentice, so I often went to the shop at night. It was stacked head-high with wooden chair frames, waiting to have a spring fixed or a cushion replaced, waiting to be covered in fake leather or clear plastic. The shop was full of sounds: the tinny music of a small radio, the buzz of a sewing machine, and the thump of a staple gun alongside the large air pump that powered it. The whole space spoke to renewal and transformation.

There was a trail through those chairs that was barely big enough to fit a body, a trail that led to a stash of the shopkeeper's dirty magazines in the back. Large upholstery needles arched like talons into a piece of foam used as a pincushion. Bolts of fabric leaned against the wall like the trunks of cut trees.

The shop was like a church for chairs — full of brokenness and resurrection, piercing things and uncomfortable realities.

Maybe that's why Lawrence felt at ease coming to the shop and saying things there that he didn't say elsewhere, the air always pregnant with a "maybe." Maybe he was flirting. Maybe not. If he went too far, maybe that would be okay. Maybe he was being mocked. Maybe he was being entertaining. Maybe, just maybe. He knew the things he was saying were dangerous, because just being himself was dangerous. He was operating outside the rules.

It wasn't the fact as much as the flaunting that raised folks' hackles. There had always been dandies, men folks snickered about, men whose wives they pitied. But at least those men put forth an effort to bring their behavior in line with their anatomy, no matter the damage repression did to their soul.

But not Lawrence. He wouldn't pretend. He wouldn't hide. And that is what people found repulsive. It was what they saw as his surrender to a lurid impulse, his embrace of an ignoble identity. The scent of a demon on his breath. Dangerous.

At my age, even I was confused by him. Even I, who now occasionally wrestled with hints of feelings he seemed to embrace. In my mind, I was a mile apart from him. Lawrence seemed to want to abdicate masculinity, slough it off like a feather from a molting chicken. I wanted to accrue it. He had given up on girls. I wouldn't. I couldn't.

For me, attractions were fluid, not set like they were for other people, not like they were for Lawrence. In me, alternating impulses came in waves — not short, rapid waves like water sloshing about in a bucket, but in great oceanic waves in which one dominated during the day and drowned out the other, which sometimes came at night, the way the betrayal had come.

It's not that I didn't also think about girls and women at night. I did, compulsively. They were girls from school and women from the dirty magazines, smiling and naked, full of praise and empty of judgment. It's just that the male images sometimes came in their stead, but not in the same way. They were a presence. A wistfulness. Yearning spirits lingering near the place where a life was once lost. They were faceless and without form, no one I knew and not naked like the women, but definitely male. They were not aggressive, but rather an amalgamation of all the men who had ever been nice to me, soothing, antidotes to the boy who had tried to take advantage of me. The nighttime images embodied the opposite of the feeling I had about what Chester had done.

To me, in my ignorance, Lawrence represented the full gender deviance of which boys are taught to want no part — kind feeding on kind. My mind was so caught between Bible verses and vicious boys — prey and predator, right and wrong, large and small, life and death — that I was incapable of seeing love or tenderness or caring in what Lawrence felt.

The thing that came to me in whispers and waves seemed to come to Lawrence with the force of whitewater rapids — churning, irrepressible, able to push you over and drag you under. Everything about him hinted at sex — coquettish manner, agreeable glances, a door that would swing wide open with the slightest push. Lawrence couldn't *not* flirt. Rivers must move. He could be still for only so long, danger or no.

The shop was the only place besides church where I saw Lawrence

talk to a man. Most men steered clear of him lest folks grow suspicious that they were drawing pleasure from exchanging pleasantries.
"How you doing?" That was it. Move on. Barely wait long enough to
receive the answer. But there among the dead chairs, Lawrence came
alive. There he didn't shrink; he blossomed.

As far as I could tell, the cousin who kept the upholstery shop was
completely uninterested in Lawrence, although entertained by him.
The "maybe" Lawrence floated in the air the shopkeeper gently but
firmly brought back to earth with a solid "no." It just seemed to me
that, as a man who had seen the cruelty of war up close, he had no
desire to be cruel to a man who posed no threat.

I would be grown before I recognized how much courage it must
have taken for Lawrence to live as he did, outside the rules and ahead
of his time in such a small place.

But not every man was like the shopkeeper. One day — more than
a decade later — the danger of Lawrence's life would catch up to him.
He would be found murdered in a neighboring town, tied to a bed.
Although I didn't know anyone in Gibsland who had ever seen him
with a man, not in a romantic way, many folks assumed that some of
the men who scoffed at him by day played around with him at night.

The gossip was that it was one of those men who killed Lawrence,
but no one knew who did it and few other than his family, particularly Aunt Trudy, really seemed to want to know. His death reduced
her bark to a whimper and shook her faith: "I don't know why God let
that happen to Lawrence. I just can't pray right no mo'." My heart hurt
for her. How could this have happened to Lawrence, the most harmless
and most isolated of men? And why weren't more people upset and
unsettled?

People whispered, but no one protested. The sense of scandal
seemed to outweigh the sense of outrage. Yet everyone went to the
funeral, many no doubt to see if a strange man turned up who looked
too hurt or cried too hard — a distraught lover or a guilty one.

The unspoken message this sent was horrible and unmistakable:

black men who lived their lives as Lawrence had lived his would not be fully valued in life or in death. The world that judged Lawrence's honest life as dishonorable would in fact conduct itself dishonorably in his death. A few people were questioned in Lawrence's murder, but no one was arrested, and soon the whole thing faded away.

Five years after Lawrence was tied to the bed and killed, Matthew Shepard, a young, white, openly gay man, was tied to a fence and killed in a small Wyoming city. While Lawrence's death hardly made the local papers, Matthew's provoked an international outcry. That discrepancy would haunt me.

My friend Shane was not like Lawrence. He didn't talk slick. Nothing he said sounded like flirting. There was no "maybe" in the air when he spoke. But he still upset the prevailing ethos: that boys from the sticks were hard like stones. What hung on Shane was a thick sense of eccentricity and erudition.

The suspicion surrounding him was not about what he said, but what he didn't say — sins of omission. He never spoke of girls, ever. Other boys talked about the pretty one or the ugly one, the fine ones or the fat ones. But Shane never did. He liked to play word games and talk trivia, which he could do for hours, and few could match wits with him. But I knew that this, too, was dangerous. It was words and reading that had made me quiet, and being quiet had made me a mark. Quiet was fine for old folks on porches, but not for young boys.

Sometimes we played basketball, and Shane was one of the best basketball players I knew. But the way he played was different from other boys. He was somehow able to use his oddly distributed weight to his advantage, contorting his body — moving loose and squirmy through the air when he jumped, the way a cat does when it falls — and taking unorthodox shots that somehow seemed to fall into the basket. He could prove his superiority, both intellectual and athletic, as often as it was challenged.

But perhaps the most inspiring thing about Shane was that he seemed able to insulate his sense of identity. He knew the things that people said about him, but he appeared not to care. He had found a way to hold himself safe and apart — looking down on the cruel ignorance of the world around him, laughing at the idea that others thought they could look down on him.

This was interesting, for a while. I needed the break. But while Shane may have grown accustomed to his isolation, I could not. Soon Shane moved away, and I moved on.

The only other person I knew with Shane's fortitude was a girl who arrived in the neighborhood a few months after Shane moved out, a girl with a strange name, Nevaeh — heaven spelled backward.

Nevaeh's family moved into a house less than a hundred feet from where Shane had lived, and they rented out the vacant municipal building across the street. The father, a missionary of sorts, started preaching and having "church" there for a strange new religion called Nation of Yahweh. This was unheard of in our town, a blasphemy. People whispered, and drove by slowly, looking in at the nearly empty services through the open door.

Nevaeh was a clever, imaginative girl and was covered head to toe in eczema. She was an outsider, not so pretty, and, the way folks told it, her parents were headed straight to hell, but I didn't care. I was instantly, magnetically drawn to her. The other kids mocked and teased her. But, like Shane, she was resilient, standing like a flower at the edge of a cesspool. The insults she didn't ignore she volleyed with a quick wit. I was drawn to anyone who didn't buckle in the face of ridicule. It was a skill I needed to acquire.

We'd sit for hours on her porch swing, moving just enough to hear the chains creak, talking about imagination and clouds and if-I-hads, everything and nothing — beautiful thoughts flowing effortlessly from her scarred body.

One day she took me into the municipal building, where her father was preparing for his next sermon. Unbeknownst to me, she was delivering me for conversion. Strange charts and illustrations hung every-where. Her father asked me if I knew who Yahweh was. I knew that the God of the Old Testament was called Yahweh, but this seemed differ-ent. Was he talking about my Yahweh or his? I was overthinking it. I said no.

He launched into a bizarre speech about a black messiah, true Jews, and the lost tribes of Israel. He talked about how the Υ's formed by the splitting of branches and the veins of leaves were subtle manifestations of Yahweh. He had me spread my fingers like his fingers, two on either side, like the Vulcan greeting on *Star Trek*.

"See that? That's a Υ for Yahweh." I thought, No, that's a V. But I said nothing.

He seemed like a pleasant man, but his logic was laughable to me, trivial, especially in light of the fire-and-brimstone, blood-and-sacri-fice, help-us-please-Savior message that had been drilled into me since I was a sprout. I knew who Jesus was, I thought. He was a white man with stringy yellow hair and blue eyes, notwithstanding the Bible's hair-of-wool, feet-of-bronze description.

I told my mother about where I'd been that day and the strange things that the strange man had said. She directed me, in no uncertain terms, to "stay away from down there!" My mother was right. Years later, the cult's founder and leader, Yahweh ben Yahweh, would be convicted in Miami of conspiring to murder white folks as part of an initiation rite.

Within months, the strange man and his daughter, unable to find willing converts or a warm reception, moved away, like Shane's family.

Having spent so much time with a girl, and before that a boy who folks thought acted too much like a girl, I was now feeling the need to rejoin the fray of the other boys.

If Shane and Nevaeh were at one end of the spectrum, the Sparrow children were at the other. They lived down the block where the street met the highway, near the upholstery shop where Lawrence came to talk slick before someone tied him to a bed and took his life. There were three of them — two boys with a girl in between. They lived in an aging trailer where my father, after he and my mother split, often spent all evening getting drunk.

The Sparrows were an unruly bunch. The older boy would hold his sister down and kiss her in response to the slightest dare. I got the sense that her protests had lost their force, that she had resigned herself to a trapped life with nowhere to run. In fact, she was the star — or victim — of the first sex tape I experienced. It was a cassette audiotape of several neighborhood boys crowding around a bed about to have sex with her.

The boys taunted and prodded her.

"Gul, take dem big-ass pannies off."

She pleaded for time to consider the act.

"Wait a minit! Wait a minit! Let me thank! Let me thank!"

The tape stopped before the action started, but start it did. The boys couldn't have been more than twelve or thirteen at the time, and she was even younger.

Sometimes I played with the Sparrow children, in part because there were only a handful of families on our street with children. We stayed in their yard while their folks and company talked, gambled, and drank inside, the air always charged with a hint of danger and the possibility of disaster. One evening, a well-liquored woman with shaky footing stumbled out of the house. She folded herself into her car and turned the ignition, and the car lurched forward. It sped through the yard, across the highway, and into a ditch, then slammed into a railroad embankment.

The train tracks, which ran through town along its northern edge and on to the interchange at the center of town, had turned 1890s Gibsland into a booming shipping center. Paradoxically, Interstate 20, opened in the early 1960s less than a mile north of the tracks, now threatened to choke the town to death by diverting through traffic. The tracks themselves had become a nuisance and a hazard, taking a life or two every few years from those who snaked around the crossing arms — at the one level crossing that had them — assuming that they'd malfunctioned, as they often did, or from those who failed to heed them.

But this was the first time I knew the tracks to threaten a life without the help of the train, and the only time I'd seen it happen in front of me.

The adults ran screaming to rescue the woman in the ditch as we ran behind them.

"Git some candy! Git some candy! She got da suga'!" They searched, but no candy could be found, at least not in time. She'd had a diabetic seizure and died in the ditch.

It was all too much for me. I never played at the Sparrow house again.

Seeking a middle ground between the taint of ostracism at Shane's and Nevaeh's houses and the air of calamity at the Sparrows', I started to play at the home of the children over the hill. One of them, a boy with two first names, Sam Robert, became my new best friend. He looked the way my father must have looked as a boy — same dark brown skin, same head of big, wet-looking curls. Only this boy walked with a wobble, like his legs didn't fit right at the hip, and his teeth were stacked like some of the permanent ones had insisted on coming in before the baby ones fell out.

He was the second oldest of six children — most with different daddies — and he was one year older than me. His family had even less than mine did: rubber balls with leaky valves, naked dolls with lazy eyes. The children were born to a toothless, canned-beer-swigging woman who didn't work and yelled profanities when she was sober enough to talk straight. "I done pushed six muthafuckas out my ass! I'm grown." "Can't nobody tell me shit! I tell you what to do." "Sit yo' ass down somewhere!" She was a West End woman.

Their house was unpainted and sat on a grass-bare, red-dirt lot with a four-foot dropoff to the street. On the side of the house was a pine tree under which we all sat and talked. On occasion we went inside and watched the family's static-plagued black-and-white television in the front bedroom, which was dominated by a squeaky bed that reeked of piss and sadness.

Sam Robert looked after his younger brothers and sisters most days, a responsibility his mother often shirked. I deeply respected him for this. I think that's what drew me to him — a boy who looked like my father but did the right thing by children.

But a boy of his age could only be so vigilant. One day, one of his little sisters was riding shotgun on a bike while wearing no shoes, and the toes of one of her feet got caught in the spokes and were ripped off — the great toe and a couple of lesser ones. We rushed to tell her mother as the girl lay in the street, in shock, silent, not even crying. Her mother ran from the house, yelling and cursing. She grabbed the girl and the ripped-off toes, begged a ride from a man in a nearby truck, and sped away to the hospital, hoping that something could be done. Of course, there was nothing that could be done.

I pretty much stayed at Sam Robert's house, until one winter day when I went there and knocked on the door. "Who is it?!" the mother yelled.

"Charles," I answered. Then she said, loud enough for me to hear, "God dammit! He stay his muthafuckin' ass ova here." She said it the way a person talks tough to a door to shoo away whatever's on the other side of it — a bump in the night, a scratching cat, a bill collector before payday. I felt ashamed and embarrassed, so I ran away before the door opened and never went back.

I could find no real place for myself in the world, so I began to spend more time alone, often in the abandoned house right across the street from our own house, set between our two truck patch gardens. Years before I was born, Papa Joe had rented the small, four-room house to a couple with two children, but the children had drowned during a day of water play on Merrick Pond when the boat they were in capsized. All the other children were saved. They weren't. They never came home. The couple quickly moved out, unable to stay in a house so drained of joy. No one ever rented the house again.

The house held a certain allure, a kind of grace as it tilted and fell in on itself, like an old lady among younger ones, challenging the eye to see it as it had been, not as it now was. It was beautiful to me in that way — its tragedy notwithstanding — the way romance hangs on a building as it rots.

It was a place from which life had been withdrawn in a hurry. There were things from that abandoned life, large and small, still strewn about, but it was the small things that caught my attention: a broken plate; a white saucer with two blue rings near the lip, the big one twice as wide as the small; a tin cup dented on both sides. They were the things that had been touched and held long ago by now-dead children, and they beckoned me, a boy trying to find his way back to life, to touch and hold them again.

The house became my own Fortress of Solitude — like Superman's retreat — where I hid and healed and thought and played and pored over my brother's secondhand dirty magazines, their pages stiff from being exposed to the weather, mildew growing in the spines where the women spread their legs. Or I would draw portraits of people, populating my world with imaginary faces to replace real ones.

As a young child I had once drawn a black man with a necklace of bones and teeth, like the "natives" on the *Tarzan* television show, one of the only ways the show seemed to portray black people. Everyone was surprised at how well the drawing turned out, including me. I always drew from then on. It was fun, but just a hobby.

Still, I bristled every time someone said, "You're going to be an artist." The only "artist" I'd ever known was not held in high esteem. He was a black man with a Jewish name — Hammerstein — who lived down by the railroad crossing. But folks didn't call him an artist. They called him crazy. His yard on all sides was filled with house-high piles of scrap metal, and he spent his days welding the metal into spooky totems.

Folks laughed at the futility and impracticality of his undertaking. I found the towering figures beautiful, but I didn't want to be a joke like Mr. Hammerstein. So I drew mostly for my own amusement, like I was doing in the House of the Drowned Children.

The only thing I ever knew to live in that house was a young deer, which had darted from the woods and across the road in front of my father's truck, the truck clipping its back legs so that it couldn't run and could hardly stand. My father, full of liquor, loaded the deer into the truck and brought it — panicky, kicking, and wide-eyed — to our house, for us to keep as a pet, I suppose. He put the deer in the House of the Drowned Children, in one of the rooms in the back, the one with the fewest things in it. We did our best to barricade the openings where the windows used to be, but as soon as the deer's leg healed enough for it to stand, it bolted through one of the openings and back into the wild.

For me the house was neither cage nor morgue, but sanctuary — a place that shielded me from unpleasant things. I didn't want to bolt back into the world but to steal away from it. There in that house I stopped running from loneliness and embraced it. Loneliness became my truest and dearest friend, a friend who would shadow me for a lifetime. On the other side of the street, loneliness had killed Papa Joe, but on this one it kept me alive.

But the house continued to collapse until it had to be brought down, which meant I had to find a new sanctuary, another place where I could run away from the world when it felt too much for me. I took my loneliness into the forested lot between Shane's old house and our own field. There the vine-strung trees stood like pillars, tall and straight, with branches intertwined high above, giving the space an airy, sun-dappled feel like the inside of a cathedral. It was peaceful, scented with spruce and pine, and quiet save the call of distant birds, the rustling of small animals, and the occasional stampede of the horses in the large field that ran behind most of the houses on the street.

I passed the hours there, reclining on a fallen tree, sometimes even taking off all my clothes, drawing myself into greatest agreement with my surroundings. I drifted back and forth through the fog of consciousness, peacefulness overriding the pain of the bark pressing into my back and the mosquitoes nipping at my flesh.

Time ground to a halt and the trees whispered in the language of God and nature about steadfastness and resilience — gently saying that one could be constantly stirred yet not moved, bent but not broken, that a thing well grounded and deeply rooted could ever stand.

That year, when I was nine, my mother got a job teaching home economics at the high school in Gibsland, a much shorter commute. I was going back to rejoin the classmates I had left after kindergarten.

This was the first time I noticed that our town's school was attended almost entirely by black children. The year I was born was the first year our school district, like many Louisiana school districts, had been forced to desegregate its public schools, after dragging its feet for sixteen years following the Supreme Court's *Brown v. Board of Education* ruling. Louisiana had taken the ruling particularly hard because it overturned *Plessy v. Furguson,* the Louisiana case that established the legal justification for Jim Crow throughout the South. In Gibsland, the white school was combined with Coleman, the black school, to create one school system. The old Gibsland campus became the lower school — Gibsland Elementary — and the Coleman campus became the upper school — Gibsland-Coleman High School, where my mother was to teach.

Local whites were not pleased. They removed their children and bused them off to the all-white academies that were springing up to protect their children from the imaginary dangers of commingling with "coloreds." Many white teachers left as well, some even taking the textbooks with them. Only a handful of desperately poor white children remained at the Gibsland schools. In fact, white children seemed to me like ghosts in Gibsland, fleeting images seen through the windows of passing cars.

At Gibsland Elementary, I was placed in Mrs. Collins's fourth-grade class. She was a pint-sized firecracker of a woman, with short curly hair, big round glasses set wider than her face, and a thin slit of a mouth she kept well lined with red lipstick.

On the first day of class, I sat at my desk, a little nothing of a boy, lost and slumped, flickering in and out of being. She gave us a math quiz. Maybe it was the nervousness of being the new kid, but I quickly jotted down the answers and turned in the test — first.

"Whoa! That was quick. Blow, we're going to call you Speedy Gonzales." Mrs. Collins said this with a broad, approving smile, the kind that warmed you on the inside. She put her arm around me and pulled me close while she graded my paper. I got only a couple of the answers wrong.

I couldn't remember a teacher ever smiling with approval, or putting her arm around me, or praising my performance in any way. It was the first time that I felt a teacher cared about me, truly saw me, or believed in me. I never got a bad grade again. In fact, from that point on, mine were among the best grades in the class. I figured that if I always shined by my work, Mrs. Collins — and everyone else — would always be able to see me. I wanted to make her as proud of me as she seemed to be that day. And she always seemed to be.

I felt life stir in me. I'd always known that I was smart, but when the teachers at Ringgold had treated me like I wasn't, I'd lived down to their expectations.

I don't know if race was a factor, but most of the Ringgold teachers had been white, and Mrs. Collins and most of the teachers at Gibsland were black. In fact, Mrs. Collins was the first black teacher I'd had since kindergarten, and the difference seemed real. She often interrupted her scheduled lesson to talk to us about citizenship, or hygiene, or whatever she thought we needed to know to be better people — not just teaching us, but raising us.

I didn't remember hearing about Black History Month at Ringgold. President Gerald Ford had only officially recognized it in 1976, when I was in the first grade. But at Gibsland it was an event, one that opened my eyes and gave me a newfound sense of pride. It was the things that I learned had been invented by black folks — everyday things, things that I regularly saw and touched and tasted — that especially impressed me. Potato chips and peanut butter. Refrigerators and oil stoves. Straightening combs and brushes. Mops and dustpans. Lawnmowers and traffic lights. Bicycle frames and ironing boards. Those things stuck with me.

The arts teacher, a thin, elegantly turned-out woman, taught us the so-called Negro national anthem, "Lift Every Voice and Sing," with its plaintive lines and demanding low notes that wreaked havoc on my voice, which was beginning to crack early. It was the only song on which we were graded. The song spoke to me in a special way, building in me a lyrical narrative of struggling and pushing through suffering.

Sing a song full of the faith that the dark past has taught us,
Sing a song full of the hope that the present has brought us,

But of everything about Gibsland Elementary, it was being embraced by the popular boys that most changed me.

It began the summer before, when I met a boy named Russell.

That summer seemed particularly hot. We had one small air conditioner, which was in William and Robert's room. We crowded into their room all day to stay cool. My mother wanted a larger air conditioner for the living room, to liberate us. She bought it, but to install it we had to have an outlet rewired. She had an amateur electrician come one day to do the job.

The man had a son and grandson who were the same age, and my age as well, and he brought them with him. Russell was the grandson. He was a tall, muscular boy with an easygoing manner, the kind other boys were drawn to because they wanted to be like him, a jock. As the old man worked with the wires, Russell, his same-age uncle, and

I wrestled in my brothers' room, jumping from sofa to bed and back again. Strong for my age, I tossed the boys with ease. It was fun. I made friends that day. Unfortunately, the old man bungled the wiring job. Every time we touched the air conditioner, it gave us a shock.

I had not considered that Russell and his uncle would be at the school and in my grade, but they were. When lunchtime came, I saw them. There were fewer than forty children in the entire grade, and we were split into two classes. The two boys were in the other class. I had no way of knowing that Russell was one of the popular kids in the grade.

During that first lunch break, he heaped praise on me in front of everyone, for being strong and cool and tossing him and his uncle around when his grandfather was working on our wiring. I was his new friend, and that mattered. On the sheer force of his effusive recommendation, I instantly became one of the cool kids.

Another boy at Gibsland Elementary who would help change my life didn't take to me at first meeting. Alphonso was a smart and popular boy, and didn't approve of my being touted by Russell. He was thin-built, handsome, and sand-colored, with eyelashes as long as a spider's legs. He was quick-witted, and he dressed better than the other boys. He was born in Dallas, but his mother was from Gibsland and had moved back to marry a local man who'd gotten a big insurance settlement after a work accident left him with burns over most of his body.

Alphonso picked at me, prodded me, trying to provoke me. It worked. Within the first week of school, we had a fight. I had never had to fight before, and I doubt if he had either, because we just swung our fists wildly. I'm not sure if either of us even landed a punch.

As is often the case, the boy you have your first fight with becomes your best friend. He became mine.

My new friends had anointed me, and I became who they thought I was, a boy full of life. They hadn't known me when I was withdrawn, when I felt most dead. They hadn't witnessed my awkwardness. Here,

I was a blank slate. I could be whoever I said I was, whoever they wanted me to be. I could transcend my life by transforming myself. And so I did.

I also became the caulk between Russell and Alphonso — the popular jock boy and the popular smart boy.

Each day we ate our lunches quickly, went to the vending machine for candy, then headed to the playground, furnished with all-metal play equipment and paved with gravel-covered asphalt. The place was alive with giggles and screams, wisecracking and signifying.

We swung so high on the swings that the chains grew slack. We played tetherball until our hands were swollen. Beyond the playground was a baseball field with decaying bleachers where we played kickball. Occasionally we ignored the bases and played roughneck football, which I was surprisingly good at.

I realized that boys were wired to follow the strongest among them. And in this I had a genetic advantage. I was taller, faster, more agile, and stronger than most boys. And I took what nature gave me and pushed it beyond that limit. I had to be the best at everything — basketball, football, kickball, dodgeball, everything — to be the boy Russell had told everyone I was. In fact, whenever I came up short I took it as an existential threat, and willed that it would never happen again.

Around this time, whenever my mother could afford it, she took us to Shreveport's Municipal Auditorium to see the wildly popular stars of the Mid-South wrestling circuit — a bunch of washed-up football players as outlandish characters in a soap opera of good and evil, tights and testosterone, cage matches and smackdowns.

"The Big Cat" Ernie Ladd. That was the name of my favorite wrestler. Six feet nine inches tall. Over three hundred pounds. All muscle. A north Louisiana native. A Grambling graduate. A local hero.

The wrestling matches were among the only crowded events my mother would take us to after we saw a woman fall in front of a car at the Natchitoches Christmas Festival of Lights. We had been sitting on the embankment by the river listening to a band. After the last song, the crowd made its way up the hill and began crossing the street. Right in front of us was a young white couple, drunk on love and liquor, holding hands, the woman's hair blowing in the night breeze. But on the road a car was creeping through the crowd like a turtle through tall grass. The woman stumbled in front of the car, but the driver didn't see her. He continued to inch forward. The woman's boyfriend banged on the car as the woman screamed. My mother, traumatized, whisked us off to our car.

But the wrestling matches we still went to.

We got the cheapest seats, but no one yelled louder or had more fun than us. The wrestlers played on racism and patriotism, ignorance and fear, producing characters of the most exaggerated stereotypes, particularly the villains.

Kamala the Ugandan Giant, a supposed cannibal, wrestled in face and body paint and a loincloth. The Great Kabuki, wearing kumadori face paint, blew a mysterious, blinding "Asian mist" into the faces of his opponents. Abdullah the Butcher, "the Mad Man from Sudan," sadistically dug forks into his opponents' open wounds. A black man called the Junkyard Dog wore a dog collar around his neck with a chain attached. Nikita Koloff, "the Russian Nightmare," sought to prove Russian superiority. Kaffiyeh-clad Skandor Akbar, an "evil Arab," managed a stable of other heels called Devastation, Inc.

I loved these diversions. They kept my mind off Chester's betrayal. Although I only occasionally thought of it now, with every recollection it grew more sinister — his sin pushing past the possibility of forgiveness, my spirit pushing past the possibility of restitution.

In the wrestling matches, each time a character was slammed to the mat it produced a thunderclap. One night after the show, we worked our way down to the main floor so that we could touch the mat. We ran our hands across it. Someone slapped it. *Bam!* It turned out that the mat was like the skin of a large drum, pulled tight. The slightest touch produced the same sound as when one of the wrestlers was slammed into it. In a way, it was disappointing, but in another way, it was inspirational. I was realizing that a strong presentation could be constructed from whole cloth, as long as you were a good enough actor to make it believable. I vowed to channel my aversion to conflict and aggression into a mastery of it. Henceforth, my interactions with suspect guys would be marked by full-throated, bare-knuckled hostility — I wouldn't run from a threat, but into it, hard. I never wanted to be a victim again.

Like the thistle of a flower, I set up sharp defenses to protect myself. I developed a bit of a strut and an arsenal of slick comebacks, all bullshit and bluster. I avoided fights by pretending to welcome them, all the while praying no one called my bluff — a lot of "I wish he would!" when I secretly hoped he wouldn't.

I wasn't so much afraid of the battle as of the loss, which would punch a hole in my new armor. I still didn't know how to fight. I didn't know how to bob and weave. I didn't know the sting of a punch — how it jolted the skull, cracked the ribs. I didn't know how to use that pain to fuel ferocity. And I didn't get any practice at home. My mother had grown up fighting, but my brothers and I never fought. We never wrestled. We didn't even slap-fight or shadowbox.

My new façade was like a thing made of matchsticks — fragile and in constant danger of going up in flames.

It was Alphonso who taught me another way to show strength. Thanks to Mrs. Collins, I now had confirmation that I was smart. But Alphonso was smarter. He did well without trying. He taught me how to use my wits. He knew how to mark his space with his words because he was too thin to defend it with his fists.

He also knew how to reduce another boy with a look. It was the kind of look that caught you at the ankles and moved up your body like an iron, flattening you, pressing out all the air and all the confidence, until his eyes set on yours with a blank stare that your insecurities invariably read as mockery or pity or some such. Nothing nice. Then he'd look away into nowhere, just before your mouth puffed with a question or your eyes tightened with anger. He: uninterested. You: unworthy.

He knew how to look at you in a way that made you beat yourself up, so that he never had to, because he knew he couldn't. It was the kind of look that left you so wounded that every time Alphonso laughed — whether hours or days had passed — you were sure that he was laughing at you. Alphonso knew this. That's probably why he laughed all the time. I too learned to look at boys with the kind of look that made their minds play tricks on them, the kind of look that said disdain, mockery, pity, nothing nice.

I also learned something about popular children that I had never known because I had never been popular myself: they are never comfortable because they are exhausted. Staying on top is harder than getting there. They're racked with insecurities. They know that their perch isn't necessarily permanent. There is always someone waiting and wanting to snatch the crown, always someone willing to betray you in order to be you. The people by your side aren't necessarily on your side.

But exhaustion and betrayal were already things that I knew well, from my much darker days, so these new forms suited me just fine. In fact, they were easier to manage than the others.

I took what I could learn from Russell and Alphonso and combined it with the lesson I had learned from Shane: prove your superiority — both intellectual and athletic — as often as it is challenged. I now had all the tools I would ever need to ensure that I would never go unseen or unacknowledged again.

So when we finished tussling in the playground, we returned to class sweaty, disheveled, grass in our hair and stains on our knees —

happy. There was no trace of the broken boy, at least not a noticeable trace.

Just as I was learning how to overcome the deficit of feeling dead on my journey to becoming a man, I had to overcome the complexity of race to become a black man in particular. The first time I heard someone call me a nigger, it forced me to reconsider the way black men and white men dealt with each other in the world I inhabited.

My family's interactions with white folks happened mostly when we went shopping. And those encounters could be fraught. Often things went well, like when we stopped at Mr. Nolte's dry goods store, where my mother would inspect the bolts of fabric stacked in the store window like cordwood. She got a couple yards of "these" and a few swatches of "those," and she might buy me a new pair of Chuck Taylors if the eggshell white of mine was past the point of being restored by washing.

But just as often, things went sour. Pity the poor cashier who miscounted my mother's change. Nothing got my mother's dander up more than feeling she was being cheated. This was another trait she'd inherited from Mam' Grace. My mother often told us the story of how Mam' Grace's mother had one day walked ten miles to a store to shop and, upon returning home, realized that the store had shorted her a dime. She walked all the way back to the store to retrieve the dime, for the principle of it. Mam' Grace and my mother wanted all of their dimes as well.

Occasionally, white people would sell goods in the black community. There was the egg lady, an elderly white woman in an aging brown jalopy who drove door-to-door selling the eggs her hens laid. There was the man who sold bulk ice cream treats from the back of a refrigerated truck. But perhaps most memorable was the white insurance man who came by once a month to collect his premium and mark our card paid. When he appeared, Uncle Paul was transformed from a gentle old man into a scared little boy. He wrung his hat in his hands while staring at the ground and shuffling his feet. He talked to the man without ever looking at him, and he agreed with everything the man said before the man could fully get the words out.

"Yas'm."

"Yas suh. Sho nuff is a perty day. I, I . . . I thought we's gone git some rain yesdiddy."

"Nah suh. I feels jus' fine."

He had learned a language and a protocol dictated by fear and necessary for survival. Like many older black people, he suffered from a chronic reflex racism. Having heard tell of — or witnessed, or experienced — so many horrible things done at the hands of white folks, he feared most and trusted few of them.

As soon as the insurance man left, Paul's irritation bubbled up.

"That old white man always comin' 'round heh askin' questions," he'd say with a scowl.

In Gibsland, our racial role-playing was subtle and sophisticated. We had an unspoken understanding: we simply danced around each other, moving to a tune that everyone knew but no one sang — warm smiles sharing space with cold stares, public platitudes dissolving into the ugly things that found voice behind closed doors. If people learned to hate, they also learned to hide it. I never heard or saw anything overtly unpleasant in public. That is, until the first time I was called a nigger.

I was walking on Main Street and a pickup truck with a flatbed filled with white boys about my age passed by. One of them stood up when he saw me and yelled "Nigger!," the word trailing off as the truck sped by, salting the space between us with bitterness. We stared at each other until he was out of sight. I was stunned.

I had always heard the word used collegially, jovially:

"What up, my nigga?"

"That nigga crazy!"

"My nigga, my nerve, my jelly preserve."

"Nigga *please.*"

As children, we used the word playfully in nursery rhymes, like "Eeny, Meeny, Miny, Moe," to solve mini-disputes about who went first, or got the last piece of chicken, or played with the toy next.

> Eeny, meeny, miny, moe,
> Catch a nigga by the toe.
> If he hollers, let him go.
> Eeny, meeny, miny, moe.
> You. Are. It.

And, of course, there was the aunt we called Aunt Nigga, a name we relayed with love and without irony. She was the mother of the other cross-the-line cousin who walked with his wrists turned out.

I didn't realize the word was a perfect little weapon when it was in the wrong mouth — a missile that could be launched from the back of a passing truck by one boy at another. I didn't realize how well it captured and projected loathing and hostility. The only other word that stung as much was "punk." Niggers and punks. Punks and niggers — both words people spat out more than said, both now aimed at me, both hurting me more than I thought I could be hurt.

The next time I heard "nigger" used that way, it came from the only white person in our class, one of the left-behind whites who couldn't afford to attend one of the all-white academies. She was a Presbyterian, which as far as I could figure meant that she never cut her long hair and always wore long skirts. One Black History Month, the teacher called on her to answer a question. She rose nervously and said, "My daddy told me that I ain't have to learn nothin' 'bout no niggers."

That didn't go over well in a room full of black children.

Hearing that word made me reconsider everything I thought I understood about my life. The hills we drove over on our way to church, the hills that hid the oil — maybe these were the hills that would have been ours if white folks hadn't taken them from one of my great-grandpas. Or the bad white man who'd forced Great-Grandpa

Columbus to choose between the land he'd earned and the woman he loved. The white teachers in Ringgold who'd never tried to reach me when I was drifting away, but instead moved me to the slow class at the first sign of trouble, a class filled with other black children, mostly black boys.

I thought about how older black people tried to pass a fear of white men on to us. "If you don't act right, the police gone git you." "Police" was just a term of art for white men. Sometimes they dispensed with the euphemisms altogether and just said, "That white man is gone git you," pointing to any white man in sight. You could see the fear in their eyes, like they were remembering things they weren't saying. It was real, the fear was. And that is what they hated, being afraid.

I was even afraid of white Santa Claus. My father's sister, the one prone to wild exaggeration and flat-out lying who had married the almost-white preacher with the almost-white hair, convinced me one Christmas that Santa came in the night and blew black pepper into the eyes of bad little boys. And she said he'd told her that he planned to do that to me. As I started to cry, she started to laugh. From then on, I tensed up whenever I saw the white man in the red suit with the black pepper.

I could easily have followed these racial cues: that white people were to be feared, to be kept at a distance, to be fed with a long-han-dled spoon. I began to internalize this fear. I sometimes felt like the monkey in the cage at the potato farm — familiar, but strangely differ-ent, constrained as a lesser being to a small world within the greater white one. And when white people looked at me, I often felt they were doing so with jack-o'-lantern smiles — frozen and hollow with a dim light behind the eyes. I could have quietly taken my place in the covert racial warfare playing out all around me.

Luckily, I was saved from that fate by Big Mama's relationship with a white family she worked for in Arkansas — the Beales. Mrs. Sophia and Mr. Beale had a child, a boy named Cody, who had an unruly mane of sun-bleached hair. Big Mama was their housekeeper — the kind of work my mother vowed she'd never do. Big Mama also worked in the Beales' gas station and convenience store, strategically positioned at the crossroads where the road from the Bend met the highway.

Mr. Beale's store was the main store in the area, and it provided a comfortable living for his family. To me, it was an air-conditioned paradise of fats, salts, and sugars — Vienna sausages and potted meat, pork rinds and spicy peanuts, pickled cucumbers, pickled pigs' feet, and pickled eggs.

Mr. Beale was a rugged man and a heavy drinker. Many days he drove me around with him as he attended to his business. He had a beat-up pickup with a cooler full of beer next to him on the seat, from which he'd crack open fresh brews en route. He also cursed a lot. He called everything a "sumbitch." Dishonorable people, stubborn cattle, mud-stuck tires, whatever: "That sumbitch!" But he was also the kind of man who valued hard work above all else, seeing it as the best judge of character. Maybe that was why he seemed to hold Big Mama — and Jed — in high esteem.

In a way, Big Mama's relationship to the Beales was one of the most stereotypical of Southern life: a poor black woman keeping house for a well-off white family. But that fact never manifested itself to me in their behavior. I was too young to think more critically about the complexities. To me, the Beales treated our family like their own, and vice versa, so that was how I saw all of us: as one big family. Once a white man came into the store while Big Mama was behind the deli counter. He looked at her and told Mr. Beale, "I don't want no nigger cuttin' my meat." Without missing a beat, Cody, who was just a boy at the time, let the man know in no uncertain terms that if he didn't want Big Mama to slice his meat, he wasn't getting any. Cody showed the man the door.

I would be much older before I fully realized that Big Mama worked *for* the Beales and not *with* them. But it wasn't the working relationship that stood out and made the most difference to me as a young boy. It was what I registered then as their basic goodness to each other, their sense of sameness.

My family's interactions with the Beales prevented racial fear and mistrust from taking hold. There seemed to be a warmth behind their eyes — just folks like any others. The relationship between our families helped me conceive of the beauty beyond — and the humanity between — black and white. It helped to rescue me from the bitterness — not by some grand act of racial contrition, but simply by acts of human kindness.

5

Look-Away Jesus

With another year came another betrayal.

When I was ten years old Nathan graduated from high school and went away to college at Grambling. This left me alone in our shared bedroom for the first time. I couldn't stand it. There were too many bad memories in that room, crouched in the corners, waiting for night to fall, waiting to get me alone, waiting to pounce. I tried to rearrange the furniture, to point the bed in different directions, to disorient the memories of death — Mam' Grace's and my own — and the male apparitions, but it could not be done. They still stirred sometimes when the room fell dark.

I didn't want to wait for them, so I slipped away to other rooms. Sometimes I lounged in William and Robert's room to talk and debate and watch television with them, trying desperately to wedge myself into their relationship. At other times I'd gravitate to Uncle Paul's room, searching for the feeling of the simpler, more innocent times when we roamed the streets like buddies, me skipping beside him, oblivious to life's land mines.

After I'd started school, Paul no longer had the job of taking care of me, so he made his own. Every day, sunup to sundown, he chopped the thigh-high weeds that grew in the field where Papa Joe had raised his hogs — swinging a sharp blade at the end of a wooden handle back and forth like the pendulum of a clock, ticking away the time, batches of grass taking flight at the top of each motion as the blade slowed and momentarily stopped. When the day was done, he raked his cuttings into a pile and set fire to them, the green grass mixed with the dry to produce great plumes of white smoke that trailed off in the breeze.

So, at the end of the day, after school was over and the weeds were burned, after supper was eaten and baths were taken, I'd go to Uncle Paul's room and loll about as he reflected on his day of hacking weeds and doing nothing. The room was spartan and ordered, like Aunt Odessa's house. There was an oak chest of drawers and a matching dresser with a tilting mirror. On the dresser was a pipe stand and ashtray, a boar's hair shaving brush and matching soap dish, and the hat that Uncle Paul wore every day.

There was an old rocking chair in front of a homemade box that rested on the floor, kept padlocked by day, filled with pouches of tobacco, cans of snuff, bundles of pipe cleaners, and jars of coins. Uncle Paul chewed tobacco or tucked a pinch of snuff between his lip and gum, spitting the black juices into a darkened coffee can. Other times he puffed on one pipe while cleaning another, threading the pipe cleaner through the stem, slow and gentle, the forward end emerging with every thrust like a caterpillar peeking out the end of a hollow stick.

The only things on the wall were two dime-store pictures above the bed — one a print of a white Jesus looking away into nowhere, the way people do when they pretend not to see you even though you know that they do, and the other a print of a kitten with too-big eyes that looked like it was about to cry.

Uncle Paul told me wonderful, simple stories about the boy he'd been before age wrapped an old man around him. He pulled the stories through time and space and out of the side of his mouth not champing down on the bit of the pipe, its bowl bouncing as he formed the words and swinging so low that I could see the yolk-yellow glow of the embers when he drew on it. Ribbons of smoke rose from the corners of his mouth, caressed his face, then found their level in the room.

I lay on the bed, soaking it up, staring into his eyes. They were the same color as Jed's eyes — brown, a hint of gray around the edges, sunrise yellow where the whites should be. But they were different. Weary, not sweet. The skin above Jed's eyes fell soft, releasing the worries before they could stick. The skin above Paul's eyes was held tight. Paul had the kind of eyes that stepped you back rather than drew you in, the kind that belonged to a man you could know your whole life and never wholly know. You could only look a little ways into Uncle Paul's eyes before you hit a wall, sensing something held apart, locked away, like the box on the floor.

Sometimes, when the evening stretched deep into the night, I'd simply roll over on his bed and fall asleep. I felt safe there.

That is, until the night I was awakened by the feel of his hand moving across my hip, arcing the way a snake moves across a log, slow and deliberate, searching for a soft spot to come down, purposeful, not a mistake. My stomach got knotty and my skin went cold — flesh remembers things. I'd been to this sad place before, only this time it was under the chin of the kitten trying not to cry and under the gaze of look-away white Jesus trying not to see.

Without a word, before the hand found its target, I quietly got up and walked out of Paul's room and back to mine. I never slept in his room again, and neither of us ever spoke of the hand that had moved across my hip like a snake. Whereas Chester's betrayal had broken my spirit, Paul's broke my heart. And yet, I struggled to convince myself that something else had moved that hand. Not Paul. It couldn't have been him. He wouldn't have done it. It was that thing without conscience or calculation that took up in the body when the mind went quiet that moved the hand. It was that thing that ran through a sleeping body like bold mice through an empty house — the twitch of a nose, the jolt of a shoulder, the jump of a leg — movements without meaning. That's what it was. Not Paul.

I had to resort to the most useful and dangerous lesson a damaged child ever learns — how to lie to himself.

I had to make up a reason, an excuse, because there is nowhere to hide in a small house. I had to make room within the rooms, a safe place midway in the mind, behind seeing and before knowing. There I could resurrect memories and bury secrets.

That's what people in this town and in our family did with secrets. No matter what it was — not a word. No good could come of giving voice to vice. Down the hole. Better there. Pack the dirt, tight, and move on. Otherwise, we might have to deal with the emotions those secrets might stir, and emotions were tricky for us. In our family we pretended we didn't have a full range. We stuck to jokes and laughter, bravado and theatrical indignation. Have fun often; have a fight occasionally. That was it. No talk of love, or sadness, or longing, or pain. No crying, no hugging, no consoling. No "I love you," "I'm proud of you," or "I miss you." That was soft talk for babies, not boys.

The fact that we loved each other was without question, but the precious few times that I heard those words they were cloaked in a joke. That didn't satisfy. It never satisfied. I longed to hear the words said somber and straight, delivered naked and fragile.

But if a thing so treasured as love couldn't be spoken, how could I speak a thing so terrible as what Chester and Paul had done? Besides, my mother was worried enough about how I was turning out. I had learned early to read the worry in her eyes and listen for it in her voice.

One night a few years earlier, at a high school basketball game, after playing with a bunch of other boys in a corner, I'd run during a break in the game from one corner of the court to another to meet my mother, whom I saw at the concession stand. I was full of the frenetic energy that little boys draw from the company of other little boys. But as I ran, a few people snickered, I suppose at something in my gait, at the way I held my head and my hands. I heard it, though I pretended I didn't. My mother apparently heard it too, because when I reached her, all smiles and open arms, her eyes were oozing dissatisfaction and fear. She laid into me in front of everyone. "Don't you run like that!" I knew then that it scared and worried her. Knowing that those thoughts were in her head sent pulses of shame through me. I never wanted to see that look in my mother's eyes again.

Another time, I'd sent a girl a secret-admirer letter and she replied, asking me to describe myself. I wrote a list of things designed to impress, one of which was "good-looking." I didn't believe I was good-looking, but I thought it a smart thing to write down. I hid my new letter on top of the hot-water heater in the bathroom, up high, higher than I could see. It didn't occur to me that higher than I could see was eye level for my mother. So she found the letter and read it. And she laid into me again, this time for describing myself as good-looking. That was a thing girls said, not boys.

It was clear to me that she was worried I wasn't turning out right, that I was sliding down an unspeakable path to an unspeakable end. She was adopting other people's doubts. If I had any remaining thought that I might not need to keep my troubles to myself, it dried up like the morning dew. These were things that I had to learn to fold tight so that no one could read them. Even though it now seemed to me that the world was full of boys like Chester and men like Paul — the kind whose sense of right broke down in the dark and still of the night — the ones who looked at me and saw a chance, not a child.

Another such man was a college friend of Nathan's. One day toward the end of a semester, Nathan let me come to school and spend the day with him. When night fell, he, his friend, and I drove back to Gibsland. When we got back to town, my brother stopped for gas. As soon as he ducked into the store to pay for it, the friend twisted himself around in his seat to make his face square with mine.

"So, do you have a girlfriend?"

I knew exactly what he was asking and why he'd waited for my brother to leave to ask it. I knew by the way he hung on the words, by the way his lips pushed back on his teeth, the way a dog looks like it's smiling when it's about to bite. I knew by that look in his eyes — those cold, black, devil eyes that catch no spark, like the eyes of the German shepherd when he pinned me down as a child and tried to kill me.

My brother's friend wasn't asking "Which girl do you like?" He was asking "You don't like girls at all, do you?" It wasn't so much to mock me as to excite himself. I could see that he was stimulated by the idea of what he presumed would be my answer, rolling it around in his mind, savoring it, the way the tongue plays with a piece of butterscotch.

I didn't answer. Instead, tension drew up my shoulders and arched my back. Anger shot across my face. I started to breathe deeply, loudly, so that he could hear me. I crossed my arms, trying to make myself look bigger than I was, tougher. I summoned the courage of an animal trapped in a corner.

I wasn't seven anymore. I was eleven. I didn't just want his eyes off me, I wanted them out of him, clean out of his head, gobs of gooey white stuff in my hands.

He held his gaze, as if saying to me, "I see you." I held mine, saying back to him, "I see you too."

When my brother returned to the car, he glanced in the back seat and saw my face. "What's wrong with him?" His friend turned and laughed it off. "Nothin'. He just mad 'cause he ain't got no girlfriend." They both laughed. But that wasn't it. He and I both knew that he had tried me, probed something he was sure was softer than it seemed, only to find out that it was harder than he thought.

I realized that men like that would always be around, always making that same assumption — that I was in a space where rules didn't apply, where everything was easy and loose, where my boyhood body was seen as a playground for something inside them that they kept hidden and tied down, predation so shameful that even white Jesus turned away and pretended not to see.

115

And I was afraid that men like that could see the hole in me, a thing I dared not admit even to myself: that I had an aching need to be chosen, to be seen, even if the eye doing the seeing caught no spark. It was a need beyond sex, unrelated to it. It was the need of a little boy whose light flickered in and out of register, on the verge of being snuffed out.

But being seen was a far cry from sexual submission. Submission — to anyone for any reason — was neither attractive nor acceptable to me. So in that moment I embraced the fire of righteous combat emanating from my mother and absorbed by me over a decade spent at the hem of her skirt. I told myself then that never again would I go without a fight.

I decided to try God again, to give me the strength to fight the fights that I couldn't.

Luckily, Reverend Brown left Shiloh soon after my botched baptism request. He was replaced by a smaller, less intimidating preacher. So I got up the courage to walk down the aisle again, and this time, when asked if I wanted to be baptized, I said yes.

When the baptismal day, Easter Sunday, rolled around, I focused on the minutiae of the morning, carefully recording the details: The clear sky the color of a Louisiana iris petal — deep blue, a hint of purple, a spot of yellow along the edge as the sun rose. The glow of my bedroom lit through sheer curtains softly rolling in the breeze. The chirping of morning birds outside my window, occasionally interrupted by the hum and beep of passing cars. I was desperate to remember everything about the world before I went under the water, sure that whatever was down there would fundamentally and irreversibly change me.

I put on my only suit and tie and got into the car with my mother and brothers. I pressed my head against the window as the car made its way down winding roads bracketed by lush spring foliage. No one spoke.

We pulled into the church parking lot, the gravel crackling under the weight of the car, and found a space. I got out and was escorted through a back door and into a hallway. One of Grandpa Bill's brothers, Uncle Lee Arthur, was waiting there, smiling proudly. He led me to the bathroom to change into my baptismal robe — a white bed sheet to be draped over my shoulders and pinned in the front. The preacher's chatty son went into the bathroom with me and made small talk. I could hear that the service was in full swing, but I couldn't make out what was being said. It didn't matter, because I could keep up with the timing by the tone. The services were all the same — the same arc of excitement building to the same-sounding sermons:

"Good moanin', saints. Can I git a aman?!"

"The spi'it movin' in heh dis moanin' . . . Aman?!"

"Dis moanin', I would like to come to you from the [whatever] chapter of the [whichever] book of [whomever]. And the wird sed . . ."

If God was quoted speaking in the passage, it would have to be repeated at least three times.

"'And the Lawd sed . . .'"

"Y'all didn't heh me dis moanin'. 'And the Lawd sed . . .'"

"Ha! Ha! We 'bout ta have chuch in heh dis moanin'! What he say?! 'And the Lawd sed . . .'"

If the Word came from one of the more cryptic books of the Bible, a deacon would stand and shout, "Make it plain!"

Then, the same overweight woman, sitting in the same spot, would erupt into pew-tilting, Holy Ghost–inspired convulsions at the same point in the sermon — every week. It often felt like the repeat of a play, folks pretending.

But one of the more authentic people, I felt, was the pastor's wife. She suffered from vitiligo, giving her a calico complexion with ghostly splotches of pale skin overtaking the dark. "Turning white," folks called it. She sat in the choir stand, stoic and quiet as if her burdens were heavy. She stood, staring up at spirits in the rafters, spirits only she could see, and sang in a whisper-thin voice, each word laced with a meaning greater than its definition, each note honed sharp and smooth before she pushed it out. The sound was true. Not perfect, but true, the way milk is most true when it's first squeezed, before they boil out the bits that could make you stronger or kill you.

After I had slipped on the sheet, I walked out of the bathroom and the ushers lined me up behind the other children. The line was arranged from youngest to oldest, shortest to tallest. I was the oldest and tallest. Last. I was visibly nervous, so Uncle Lee Arthur tried to calm me.

"Ain't nothin' to be scared of, baby."

I recalled the story my mother had told me about her own baptism, which took place in a snake-infested creek. When she stepped into the water, shivering from fear and the chill, Uncle Lee Arthur had calmed her fears as well.

"Cain't nothin' hurt you in dis water."

The choir began to sing the old Negro spiritual "Wade in the Water," with its haunting refrain, "God's a-going to trouble the water." It recalled the Bible story of the pool at Bethesda, encircled by the infirm. As it is written: "For an angel went down at a certain season into the pool, and troubled the water: whosoever then first after the troubling of the water stepped in was made whole of whatsoever disease he had."

The pastor invited the other children, one after another, into the pool, which was up behind the choir stand and looked like a bathtub three times as deep as it should have been. The pastor stood waist-deep in the pool, draped in a full pastoral robe, which floated beneath the water like fabric that had caught a breeze and got stuck midflutter. He prayed and marked the moment with a proclamation about another soul being delivered to God.

I wanted to be made whole, but I was still afraid of whatever spirit was in that water. I didn't want to be seized by something that would take me over, something that, holy or not, I couldn't control.

The pastor prayed and proclaimed over the boy in front of me. He put one hand on the small of the boy's back and the other on his forehead and swiftly dunked him backward into the water and brought him back up. The boy wiped the water away from his eyes and climbed out of the pool and into the arms of ushers standing with towels at the ready.

I was next. The pastor beckoned me with an outstretched hand. I slowly stepped in, trembling as I descended, the cold water rising to my chest.

I turned to see the choir and the congregation staring back at me. The pastor began to talk, but I paid no mind to what he was saying. The panic started to set in. I couldn't swim. I didn't know how to hold my breath. Was the old me really going to be washed away? And if so, who would emerge from the pool?

I felt the pastor place his hand on the small of my back. My body tensed up. He put his other hand on my forehead and, without warning, splash! I'd closed my eyes, but I could hear the pastor's murmurs through the water. It was getting in my nose! I started to kick and flail and claw at his hand. He wasn't going to drown me. Not today. He tried to hold me down, but I wouldn't be held.

I came up out of the water to see that I'd soaked the pastor head to toe and splashed nearly half the water out of the pool and into the choir stand. The choir members had scurried to opposite sides of the stand to keep from getting wet. The congregation was rolling with laughter, and my mother had hung her head.

I stared up at the pastor, and he back at me. He was not pleased. I'm not sure whether he thought I was being insolent or was possessed, but he grabbed me and dunked me again, for good measure.

Now it was done. I moved toward the steps on the other side of the pool so that I could climb out. I'd expected a spiritual transformation, a rebirth, but — nothing. I'd been under twice and I hadn't had any revelations — there was nothing down there. Maybe God had forgotten to send the angel to trouble the water. Or maybe, as with the Bible story, the first child had felt all the healing, leaving none for the rest of us. All I felt was wet and embarrassed.

I stepped out. An usher wrapped me in a towel and put his hand on my shoulder. He couldn't stop laughing.

In the silent space where I waited to hear from God, my body began to whisper, then to shout, and eventually to drown out all else.

I was eleven years old the first time I had sex with a girl, if you could call it that. Roseanne was the younger sister of a stocky boy in my class named Arthur. She was a bit taller than me, and I was going steady with her. Our relationship had come out of nowhere — the result of eyes winked, notes passed, and urges obeyed. She was very fair and a little plump and known to be sexually active — "fast," folks called it — which was a large part of my attraction to her. Roseanne was a bit dispassionate, even cold, unplugged to protect her most basic self from the poor choices she was making. I didn't mind, though. In fact, I preferred it. I, too, knew what it meant to unplug. I needed just what she was offering — the primal comfort of physical closeness without the emotional complexity of true connection. Her coldness gave me succor, the way pressing a cheek to a cold window can draw down a headache or relieve anxiety.

Her scent was an intriguing blend of hormones, sweat, and cheap perfume, and her forwardness was like a beacon. She had full lips, the color of Ruby Red grapefruit, with which she taught me to French kiss without ever taking the gum out of her mouth. It was my first real kiss. It made something explode inside me, every nerve going tingly, like being tickled and fed ice cream and having the back of your neck rubbed where the head meets the muscle, all at the same time — the manifestation of "more!"

On bus rides home from school, Roseanne and I sat together like the other couples who "went together," kissing and groping, while other kids joked and laughed, teased and harassed, tried to nail the lines to "Rapper's Delight," and sung their own wry rhymes.

What's da matta wit yo' Afro, niggero?
Dat stuff will neva grow.
Look at mine, it's so fine,
I comb it all the time.
Afro sheen and Vaseline
Dat stuff won't do a thing.
Gitta rake, gitta rake,
Gitta rake, gitta rake.

I got off the bus at Roseanne's house. Her parents never seemed to be home, which gave her and Arthur time and space to experiment. Arthur was often in the company of a small girl with a toothy grin and a glint of devilment who seemed incessantly entertained by her own promiscuity, much like Arthur himself. The girl bragged and laughed about her many sex acts, but each explicit tale and each cackle seemed to me laced with sadness, the kind that haunts you when night falls and you are alone with yourself.

Roseanne and Arthur's lack of supervision was more the rule than the exception. Since there were few jobs in Gibsland, most parents worked in neighboring towns and most kids had no parents at home after school. Which meant that in the afternoons Gibsland was almost entirely populated by handfuls of old people and hordes of restless young ones.

Little boys with bare feet and scraped knees scooped crawdads from the red-silt bottoms of tiny streams, the same streams that crawled over their banks and into the streets when a thunderstorm came calling, dropping rain faster than the earth could drink it. Other boys zipped through the streets on pieced-together bicycles, drawing adrenaline from fear in order to outrun vicious dogs that sprang from beneath rotting steps. Sandlot basketball games stretched from afternoon into night, played by glistening boys in grass-worn yards, clouds of orange dust at their feet, shots falling through warped bicycle rims nailed to leaning trees.

Pretty girls, precisely groomed in short-shorts and tight shirts, posed in cool places, showcasing an awareness, but not a command, of budding sexuality. They had just begun to use makeup — "painting," folks called it — so they still applied it with a heavy hand: too much blue on the lids, too much pink in the cheeks.

Young men perched over oily motors under open hoods, trying to resuscitate hot rods, with the ghosts of skid marks, speeding tickets, and back-seat romps still exciting the imagination. Silky young women floated about in cotton dresses that caught the sun but released the heat.

The culture we were all adrift in was steeped in a kind of premature sexualization. From the time a boy was old enough to leave home on his own and get out of earshot of womenfolk he was peppered with questions: Who's your girlfriend? How many girlfriends do you have? Are you "gittin' some"? If you had no girlfriend or weren't getting any, the old men under the shade trees were quick to offer their assessment: "There's something wrong with that boy."

One day after school, Roseanne and I sat in her living room. It was hot, so she left the front door open. She asked what I wanted to do. I knew she was asking about sex. Unable to muster the courage to speak the words, I pointed to a poster of the rock band KISS on the wall. Soon we were locked in an embrace, kissing and sliding off the sofa and onto the floor in front of the open door. She stopped, got up, and led me to her bedroom. The room was tiny and smelled like her. I was nervous and excited.

She lay on the bed and pulled down her pants. I pulled down my pants and lay on top of her. I had no idea what I was doing — how to get the parts to where they were supposed to be or how to move when they got there. I had only seen sex as still images in the mold-filled magazines in the House of the Drowned Children and at the back of the upholstery shop, where one cousin hid from his family and another came to talk slick. My body never entered Roseanne's. She stared up at me with a look of disappointment and disapproval. She was accustomed to boys who knew what they were doing.

Before I could figure things out, the phone rang and she got up and answered it. It may have been her mother. Still nervous and excited, I didn't even wait for her to return. I pulled up my pants and left. I ran home, skipping, drawing one knee up high while stretching the opposite arm toward the sky like I was about to take flight, switching to the other knee and arm every time gravity pulled me down.

Little did I know that my lack of know-how meant that the relationship was over. The next day, Roseanne and her friends sneered and laughed at me. I was eleven years old and didn't even know how to "do it." That was pathetic.

I lost the girl, but I learned a lesson — about myself. The impulses within me were not of equal weight and didn't share space. Attraction for me seemed to be a zero-sum game. The more I was into a girl, the less often the male images came. Those images weren't completely gone, however. They were still there, floating around in the back of my mind, light and loose, like the seeds of a dandelion. But they were diminished and seemed of less consequence.

Learning this was both blessing and curse. It clouded things, this idea that love could be not only an ephemeral opiate but also a practical tool. It could amplify some impulses and tamp down others. From now on I would question my affections: Was I truly falling in love or manufacturing it? Was I allowing myself to be used by love or using love? Would all the great loves of my life be the whole truth or half a lie?

6

Change

The next year, seventh grade, was marked by a torrent of change in my life.

I was now on the Coleman campus, which had begun its life in 1887 not as a high school but as Coleman College, the first black college in the region, founded to educate the children of freed slaves.

In 1915, a few months before he died, Booker T. Washington visited Coleman and held a public rally. At the rally, the white mayor of Gibsland at the time, a man with the family name Lazarus, summarized the mission of the school and its founder: "There has never been any race trouble since Coleman came to this community. Coleman is to us all a guarantee of peace between the two races. Coleman has taken raw, gawky, unpromising country boys and made men of them."

The school I knew, without ever articulating it as such, seemed still to be in that business — mitigating racial strife among grown folks and raising character in young ones — although it wasn't nearly as impressive in appearance as it had once been. The original Victorian study halls and dormitories, built in part with money from salaries the staff refused to take, had long since vanished. Our incarnation was a sprawling, uninspired building made of painted cinderblock.

The school did, however, occupy its original imposing site, stretched along a horseshoe-shaped ridge on top of a hill. A historian once described the ridge as being "made by the hand of nature's God" on "one of the most picturesque hills in the state." And, traditionally, there was a certain elegance in the way "Coleman kids" comported themselves, a dignity and restraint in the way they dressed and acted, a holdover from the school's college days.

But not only had my school changed, my perception of the culture around me and my view of myself within it were changing too. People who looked like me — chocolate brown — began to vanish from popular black culture, and I lost some of the pride I had been taught, in ways both explicit and implicit, to have in myself.

Maybe it was the defiant Afro succumbing to the greasy Jheri curl, or the debut of the racially ambiguous, girl-crush juggernaut R&B band Debarge, or the beginning of the improbable metamorphosis of Michael Jackson from a black boy into what looked like a white man. Maybe it was the end of the shows my mother watched with us when we shucked corn and shelled peas — *Sanford and Son, Good Times,* and *What's Happening!!* — everyday-struggle sitcoms starring everyday-looking black people.

The cultural currency of skin tone had shifted. The pendulum had swung back from the black-is-beautiful 1970s. "Bright" skin. Light eyes. "Good" hair. Having any one of those was now a plus. Having two was better. Having all three was the color-struck trifecta. Black, as I knew it, and as I was, no longer seemed beautiful. I had mostly dodged the racial war, but now found myself in an intraracial one. No one wanted sugar from Chocolate anymore. This was a new day, an age of more lightening cream and less Afrosheen. The Black Power of the 1960s and '70s was being crushed into a beige powder.

Whenever dark-skinned blacks appeared on television, they were assimilators, cast in fish-out-of-water sitcoms as back-talking butlers and maids (*Benson* and *Gimme a Break!*), irascible orphans (*Diff'rent Strokes* and *Webster*), and new-money up-from-nothings (*The Jeffersons*). And they were surrounded by all-white casts, like bubble wrap, I assumed to cushion the impact of their presence.

But as I grew less confident in my skin, I grew more confident in my intelligence. The school district sent a man to give IQ tests to the smartest children at our school. It turned out that, far from being "slow," as the teachers at Ringgold had labeled me, I was "gifted." Another boy, one grade up, and I tested so high that the district sent a teacher to our school once a week to teach just the two of us.

Meanwhile, in my family, Big Mama slowly eased back into herself, becoming less explosive, as time soothed the pain of losing Jed. Grandpa Bill moved on from his marriage to his young wife and moved into a new house.

My mother was also changing. She was settling down. She still took night classes avidly, but the gun learned to stay home and the brass knuckles disappeared from the glove box. And she found a man, the father of one of my classmates, a long-haul trucker who treated her well and didn't ask for much. There was no more scavenging. People could still push her buttons, but there were no more car chases and no more shooting.

Even my father was trying to be a better man. He slacked off carousing and skirt-chasing. Instead of coming in the night to deliver false promises on liquored breath, he came to leave penance, food my mother would sort through when morning came. A load of melons. A basket of tomatoes. A few bushels of greens. Anything he'd come by. It was an interesting act of compensation, leaving nourishment for children starved of his affection. It was the way of a man who needed to say something simple that he couldn't say simply: I'm sorry.

It was during this period that I finally found something I would be able to cling to as evidence of my father's love.

When the Commodore 64 computer debuted in 1982, I convinced

myself that I had to have it. A few years passed, the price fell, and Kmart marked it down, but it was still out of my mother's price range. I decided to earn the money myself. I mowed every yard I could find that summer, for $10 to $15 each, but it still wasn't enough — the grass just didn't grow that fast. So my dad agreed to help me raise the rest of the money by taking me to one of the watermelon farms in Saline — "the Watermelon Capital of the World," near where my great-grandfather landed after he ran from the Alabama white tops — to load up his truck with wholesale melons and drive me around to sell them.

He came for me before daybreak. I climbed into the truck, littered with months-old coffee cups, dirty papers, and random tools, and reeking of cigar smoke and motor oil. We made small talk, nothing much, but it didn't matter. The fact that he was talking to me was all that mattered. We arrived at the farm, negotiated a price for a truckload, and fussed over the melons we'd take. We loaded them, each one seemingly heavier than the last, and we were off.

I had never before spent time alone with my father. It felt great. We drove north to Arcadia, where we spent the afternoon selling watermelons to his friends. I got to see a small slice of his life — poolrooms, liquor stores, and loose women's houses. People smiled when he drove up. They made jokes, many at his expense. He smiled and laughed and repeatedly introduced me as "my boy," a phrase he relayed with a palpable sense of pride. We didn't get back home until dark. It was one of the best days of my life. Although my father had never told me he loved me, I would cling to this day as the best evidence of that love.

I was now old enough to know that he had never intended me any wrong. He just didn't know how to love me right. He wasn't a mean man. I never once saw him angry. I don't even think that he was angry the night he and my mother fought. His crime and his cruelty were the withholding of affection, not out of malice but by blind indifference, which I suspected grew out of his own brokenness. In a way we were not so different, he and I, both stumbling through life trying to find our footing.

So I took the random episodes of engagement—especially this day—and held them safe like a thing most precious, squirreling them away for the long stretches of coldness when a warm memory would prove most useful. I did with his affection what Aunt Odessa had done with the money in the Wonder Bread bags.

"My boy."

Perhaps the greatest change in my life was that I was coming to better understand what was happening within me. Time was adding flesh to the male apparitions that sometimes came in the night. They now had faces. Not distinct bodies, but faces. They were not men I knew personally, or even men as I knew them to look—leather-faced and wrinkle-etched, a look that bespoke a life filled with cold beer, devoted women, and grueling work. Instead, they were men from TV or magazines—slight, sedate, a tad too pretty, with gentle eyes and wide smiles, nonthreatening and not entirely unlike the women.

And the timing of the visits became more predictable. The male figures came when my world slowed down—when school was out or basketball season was over—and when I was most lonely, either between girlfriends or squabbling with a male friend.

It was now clear that some part of this male presence, however small, was sexual. Not explicit, not intercourse, but sexual in the broadest, most ambiguous sense—affection. But how much so I couldn't measure. There was no way to appraise such an amorphous thing. It was like trying to isolate a plume of smoke in a bank of fog—impossible. But this new understanding of the male figures' meaning brought fear and frustration.

How could this be? The thing that I thought had caused the most pain, done the most damage to my spirit, was now a thing that haunted and beckoned me. I believed that, against my will, my brain was braiding together the real remnant of pain with the vaporous possibility of pleasure—or was it comfort?—like two strands of the same rope.

Some nights, when everyone was asleep, I'd slide out of bed, get the well-thumbed family Bible from the bookshelf that held my beloved encyclopedias, and turn to the index. I'd find the word, under H: homosexual. It was a word not used by anyone I knew, but one that found its way to me on a wave of television hysteria about a mysterious new "homosexual cancer": AIDS — a strange name, I thought, for such a scary thing. I didn't know any big words to describe the whole of me, only small ones: torn, cloven, split like the hooves of a hog. So I looked up the big word I knew, the one of which I was most afraid, and I followed the page number to the passage.

Leviticus, chapter 18, verse 22: Thou shalt not lie with mankind, as with womankind: it is abomination.

I wasn't lying with anyone, particularly not other boys, but I wanted the part of me that was conjuring the male figures gone, forever. It wouldn't go. Even when I found myself most attracted to girls, I knew that the male figures were still there, lurking somewhere behind consciousness, and would soon return. Hovering. Present.

I was sure that the thing happening in my head was covered by Leviticus, even if the verse's literal language didn't apply. I also believed that thinking something was as bad as doing it. And, since there was no way for me to entirely control something so evanescent, the way it came and went on a whim, I believed there was no way for me not to sin. And, by extension, that there was nowhere for me to go but hell. "Abomination."

I decided that if my mind wouldn't fully follow chapter 18, verse 22, I'd force my body to follow all the other rules in that chapter. Surely God would give me credit.

I read the book of Leviticus from front to back and started to follow every rule I saw as best I could. The change most notable to my family was that I no longer ate pork and catfish. Leviticus 11. This went on for months, and I felt a strange sense of pride in my accomplishment, my ability to change my behavior. But my mother grew worried, so much so that she had a local preacher's wife, a fellow teacher, call me to explain that I didn't have to follow all those rules in that way, something about what Jesus had done, fulfilling the laws or some such.

So I stopped. But still I was proud. I felt that I'd done something positive, even if I'd been misguided, and I believed that God appreciated the effort. But I still wasn't a born-again Christian. One evening I decided to change that.

I remembered a simple prayer that I'd heard a televangelist recite, and I got down on my knees and recited it myself. I confessed my sins, admitted that I could no longer handle my life on my own, and asked Jesus to step in to guide me. That was it. Then I got up and walked outside and watched the light stoop down behind the hills. It was the time of day when the orange glow of the setting sun brushed the tips of the tallest trees, a few lonesome rays finding openings in the thicket and falling on lucky spots in the grass. It was the time of day when the lightning bugs were just beginning to sparkle against the velvet stretches of long shadows. I felt something move through me, taking with it all the pain and the questions and depositing peace in its wake.

From that moment on, my eyes were often closed in prayer, lost in the dark serenity of my mind, luxuriating in the comfort of God's power, willingly subjugating myself to His will.

I had heard or read somewhere that Christians were supposed to meditate in the spirit. I didn't know what that meant, so I devised my own method. I'd take my bath early each night, go to my room, tune the radio to the classical music station — the way I imagined heaven must sound — and slip under the covers. I'd lie flat on my back, legs and ankles together and hands crossed over my body, like the image of the man seared on the Shroud of Turin.

I focused on clearing my mind, thinking about nothing but elemental things — air as it moved through my body, images of moving water, the stillness of peace. When I had cleared my mind, I'd imagine my spirit floating up and out of my body, above the bed, then above the house and out into a clear, serene place in the dark of space. There I would come into the presence of Jesus, not white Jesus with the stringy hair and the blue eyes, but a glowing presence, emanating light but taking no form. And there I would hover, meditating, in the presence of the spirit, waiting for instructions — not actual words but revelations. Sometimes they came, sometimes they didn't. But I was content either way.

Every day I grew stronger in my "communion with God," every day I lost more interest in the concerns of the world. No more death, no more predation, no more poverty, no more powerlessness — it all receded, all insignificant in the expanse of eternity and the immensity of God's grace. He had given me perspective and lifted my burdens. I had been set free.

I had started up with a new girlfriend just before all this happened, a cheerleader two years my junior, who sent the basketball game crowds into a frenzy when she danced the cabbage patch on the sidelines. She was a pretty girl with a graceful neck, full cheeks, and a husky singing voice.

I was afraid to tell her about my transformation, scared that she would tease me and leave me. But one of the revelations that came to me was that I must tell her. So I did. And she didn't react negatively. She was relieved. She too had recently had a similar experience and was afraid to tell me. Now we had each other, and Jesus.

I prayed everywhere. I prayed in class by putting my head on my desk and pretending to rest when my work was done. I prayed on the school bus by pretending to be asleep. I even prayed when I was playing sports, like the time I won the basketball game with my eyes closed in devotion.

I was a sophomore, on the varsity basketball team. My brother Robert was co-captain, and played center. I was a second-string point guard. The first-string point guard had fouled out, and the coach, an intense, skinny man with a little round belly and black-dyed hair that was white at the roots, put me in with just a few seconds left to play.

The fouled player from the opposing team was preparing to shoot free throws. The game was tied. I lined up on the lane, closed my eyes, and drowned out the crowd. The only sound now was the soft thud of the basketball against the hardwood. One, two, three, four — four bounces, evenly spaced.

I should have been hoping for the rebound, hoping that we could regain possession, hoping that we could score a final, winning shot or at least send the game into overtime. But I wasn't. I was praying. I was praying for God to remove from me any desire to win. I was praying for Him to help me remember that His glory and His will were all that mattered.

As I prayed, the ball bounced — one, two, three, four. There was a pause. Then *swoosh.* Score! Now the other team was up by one point. I didn't let it bother me; I intensified my prayers. "Your will be done. Your will be done."

Again came the bounces — four, evenly spaced. Then the pause, but this time a bang, then a thud. I opened my eyes to realize that the ball hadn't gone in the basket but bounced off the rim and landed right in front of me. I grabbed it and took off like a shot toward our basket. Fans jumped to their feet. The floor pounded with the weight of players in pursuit. Just as I crossed the top of the key on our end of the court, I closed my eyes again. "Your will be done. Your will be done." I released all care, all fear, all wanting. I allowed God to guide. Nothing else mattered — not the ball, not the basket. The prayers were working. I felt my soul glide away — out of my body and into the heart of God.

I have no memory of opening my eyes again, but I do remember the stretch of my body, leaping for the lay-up just as the buzzer sounded, the pebbled leather of the ball as it rolled off my fingertips. As I landed, still running, I opened my eyes and looked back over my shoulder. The ball had fallen through the basket. Score! We had won.

The crowd went crazy. I smiled. I hadn't done it, He had. "All glory be to God."

I didn't just pray for me, though. I prayed for others, too.

Big Mama came to stay with us because she had fallen ill. She passed her days in my mother's bed, unable to draw the strength to rise and walk. It wasn't clear to me how serious it was — if she might cough up lots of blood like Jed and that would be it, or if one day the bed would be made without even a wrinkle and life would be gone from the room. All I knew was that this house was running out of spaces for people to die.

I brought her case before God. While Paul was in the field cutting and burning the weeds, I slipped into his room, where I was least likely to be discovered. I walked behind the bed and fell to my knees, where my feet had landed when I'd climbed down from the bed on the night Paul's hand had moved like a snake.

In that narrow space between the bed and the wall I began to pray and moan and meditate. I stayed there for more than an hour, waiting on a word from God, a revelation. Eventually, it came. I felt God was telling me to lay my hands on Big Mama. Without questioning, I rose with stars in my eyes — they'd been held too tight for too long. I walked into my mother's room and sat on the bed. I pretended that I had simply come to talk, and I gently laid my hand on my grandmother's leg.

The next day she was up and about. In my mind, there was no doubt that God had done it. God, using my faith and my hand, had raised her. I was excited and in awe, but most of all, encouraged and affirmed in my faith.

Soon I came to believe not only that I could change the present, but that I could see the future. I knew religious folks called this ability prophecy, and superstitious folks called it "born with the veil." I would dream of a person on a deathbed with folks crowded around, the way we had crowded around Mam' Grace's bed — not a particular person, a faceless one — and soon after, whether days or weeks, someone would always die. I refused to accept this as coincidence, so submerged was I in faith and the spirit. I became so convinced that I was foretelling folks' demise in my dreams that I grew wary of going to sleep.

I became an usher at Shiloh Baptist so that I'd have an excuse to be there every time the doors opened, and I began to watch the religious channel on television. One day there was an on-air food drive to help starving children somewhere in the world. The suggested pledge was $10. Just $10 could do so much good. I had $10. In fact, $10 was all I had. I felt moved to call in and pledge it. So I did. I had heard in church that if you gave cheerfully, God would return it to you tenfold. Within a week, I had gotten nearly $100 in gifts. It was my birthday. Again, I gave God credit.

But the thing that I prayed most fervently for didn't happen. I prayed to God, the primary male figure in my mind, to remove the others, the ones that so offended Him and me. But they didn't go away, not completely. Love of God had the same effect as love of girls: it pushed them down but not out. Not even God could do what I wanted done.

I felt the spirit was telling me to go even further in my devotion, to do something I wasn't prepared to do — become a preacher. That, I decided, wasn't going to happen. As powerful an influence as religion had become in my life, I was still ashamed to acknowledge it in public. My prayers were held fiercely private. Going public as a preacher was a bit beyond.

That year I was selected as the single delegate from my school to attend the regional Hugh O'Brian Youth Leadership seminar, a cultish-feeling assembly of high achievers, big smiles, and constant affirmations, founded by an actor most famous for playing Wyatt Earp on TV. I had been elected president of my class since we started electing officers in the sixth grade — as well as being president of every club I was in — so in Gibsland, I was synonymous with leadership. This was one of the long-lasting effects of having been anointed by Russell and accepted by Alphonso.

The youth seminar convened over a weekend at a hotel near the airport in Shreveport. This was the first time I had ever been in a hotel, but I tried not to let on. Still, the rooms smelled funny, the way new things smelled, like starch and glue and paint and Kmart. And it felt sealed like the inside of a Mason jar. The air didn't move, like you could use it all up and die — no draft to flutter the curtains, no whistle as it slid between window and sill. I stayed up most of the first night paying attention to my own breathing, ready to run outside if it became labored.

We met each morning in a large conference hall to hear speakers who seemed just a little too excited, and whose job it was to stir our excitement. We had to repeat more times than I can remember: "To be enthusiastic, you must act enthusiastic!"

One day we boarded a bus and drove to Baton Rouge, the state capital.

The trip, from the hill country in the north of the state to the Cajun country in the south, came as a culture shock to me. Things looked different — cypress trees rising from black swamps and draped in Spanish moss. Folks sounded different — like they had arrived from a foreign place and only recently adopted English. Some even looked different — not black or white or mixed race as I knew it, but something else altogether: apricot-colored.

In Baton Rouge we toured the capitol, where the guide told us about Huey Long, the popular governor from a small north Louisiana town that was about as far south of Shreveport as Gibsland was east of it. He was assassinated on the eve of a presidential bid, shot in this very building. The guide pointed out the place where the bullets hit the wall. The guide also told us about Huey Long's brother Earl, also a Louisiana governor, who had once been committed by his wife to an insane asylum while he still held the office. The *New Yorker* writer A. J. Liebling described Earl Long as being "as full of hubris as a dog of ticks in spring."

Then we were taken to the governor's mansion to meet the current occupant. We filed into one of the house's receiving rooms, and shortly afterward in strode the diminutive, cocksure Edwin Edwards, our corrupt, philandering, gambling governor. Two years before, on the verge of one of his comeback elections, he had boasted, "The only way I can lose this election is if I'm caught in bed with either a dead girl or a live boy." His flamboyance, his flouting of authority, and his "can't catch me" gingerbread-man act fit with the state's legacy of good-hearted, bad-boy governors and endeared him to voters, who had a long love affair with impudence. Edwards thought himself untouchable, and his swagger conveyed as much.

My mother was a huge Edwards fan. He was a rascal and a fighter. I had learned long ago that she was partial to tilted men, those with a bit of devilment, those like my father and hers. I knew from the moment I saw Edwards that I wanted to be him, the kind of man my mother admired.

In fact, part of me felt that fate may have been aiming me in that direction all along. Even with all my class and club presidencies, I had never thought of leadership as a viable career. In Gibsland, being an elected official was something people did on the side, in addition to their day job. But that day, in that moment, something just clicked: I was going to be the governor of Louisiana.

That afternoon we sat on the fresh-cut grass under tall trees near the mansion. As we ate jambalaya a Creole caterer had made in a vat in the back of his truck, I thought about the future in a way I had never done before, confident that I had finally figured out what I wanted to do with my life, what I was meant to do with it.

This was the first time I was forced to think critically about the choices my family had made — the shooting, the scavenging, and the bad thing that Uncle Henry had done, whatever it was — the many choices that would not reflect well on a boy who wanted to be a better person and a public figure. I knew then that I would have to separate the bad bits from the good, like debris from dry beans, and hold on only to the parts that I found agreeable. My love for my family would have to live separately from what I was sure would be other folks' judgments about them.

I knew that I probably wasn't suited to be a preacher who forever enforced the rules, but was more suited to be like the governor who occasionally bent them. But having political aspirations meant I needed to tell the spirit in my head "No." After that, it vacated, the revelations ceased, and the peace lifted. In fact, all feeling went with it. I stopped dreaming entirely. When I closed my eyes I met the darkness uninterrupted until daylight came again, completing the journey from drowsiness to wakefulness, all through a tunnel of nothingness, emerging not truly rested, only aware that time had passed. No mysteries to ponder or decipher. Nothing. Just doing as my body dictated, feeling that I existed apart from it.

Perhaps the most unsettling change for me was that I could no longer cry, at least not for the most part. My tears had been taken from me once before, in the wake of Chester's betrayal, and now it happened again. I was bottoming out, emotionally, all over again.

This became most apparent during two funerals I attended, back to back, at which I thought that I would collapse in tears, but none came. The first was the funeral of four children murdered by their mother.

Their father was a local boy who had lived down past the segregated cemetery and just shy of the hill where Bonnie and Clyde were killed. He had married the woman and moved to South Carolina. But there was a darkness in the woman. As a child, she was convinced that her own mother, who died of heart failure, had killed herself because the mother's heart wasn't big enough to love her. This sent her careening from mental institutions to foster homes. When she grew up and became a mother herself, she became convinced that she too was about to die. So, to protect her children from the pain she had felt when her mother died, she drugged the children, put them in an upstairs bedroom, wired the door shut, and burned the house down. The oldest child was six years old. The youngest was eight months.

The woman showed up for her arraignment in a trance, the magistrate said. She muttered only two words, in the weak voice of a woman who'd done a truly bad thing: "I'm tired." The forensic psychologist testified, "She protected her children by putting them to sleep and in the hands of God." God brought the babies home to Gibsland to be sent on to glory.

The funeral was held near my house, in a municipal building across a vacant lot from the house where the eczema-covered girl's father had tried to induct me into the cult that conspired to kill white people. The building was relatively new and built like a church — wheat-colored brick on a concrete slab, with pews, a pulpit, a choir stand, and a baptismal pool. But the only times it was used was for weddings and funerals when the person's home church was too small to hold the crowd, and by an elderly music teacher who organized an annual spring play there, until she was killed when her car was hit by a train at the crossing.

I arrived on time for the funeral, which meant that I was late. This was expected to be a spectacle, so people had come early. The ushers sent me through one of the back doors to the choir stand, where there were a few seats still available. As I went up on the stand I stared down at the tiny caskets. Four. Interspersed with flowers. Stretching all the way from one side of the building to the other. I had seen a casket as small as these only once before, when I was a little boy, in the old church in Shiloh, after the death angel had dipped into the crib and taken a baby cousin.

I took a seat facing one of the children's uncles, who was in the first pew. He was a boxy boy who played on the basketball team with me. I had never seen him cry before, but that day he was bent over with sadness, inconsolable. In fact, there wasn't a dry eye in the building except mine.

I was embarrassed. The thing that stirred other folks' souls no longer stirred mine. So I soon got up and left, pretending to be overcome, knowing everyone would understand. I walked around outside among the quiet cars, which were pointing at the building from all directions.

I wondered what was wrong with me, wondered what had happened to the heart I once had. Then I thought about the only thing that I was sure would make me cry, the death of the only person in the world who I was sure loved me: my mother. The thought of her dying and leaving me all alone reduced me to tears and reminded me that I was still human, still alive.

The other funeral was for our basketball coach. He had a heart attack and died one night after a parent-teacher conference during which an irate parent yelled at him.

The coach had struggled with us, trying, in the way good coaches do, to make better men as well as better athletes of us. He yelled a lot and often twisted his words: "Dat's why y'all can't run no damn where — smokin' dat wine and drankin' dat dope!"

He was right, of course, if a little backward in the phrasing. Everyone was drinking and smoking, it seemed, except me. I shared a locker with Russell and Alphonso, regular drinkers who stocked the locker with bags of weed. They smoked, and I didn't. No pressure, no judgment either way. We had an understanding. But in truth, I could not fully rid of judgment the eye I was turning.

The coach had tried to work with me to improve my passion for the game. I had the talent but not the heart. I was now as tall as my brothers, but as a result of always being the smallest when we played sandlot ball, I'd gotten good at dribbling around outside while they'd post up down low. Playing point guard came naturally now. I was able to see the movements on the floor as if they were being diagrammed on a clipboard, able to handle the ball as if it were a natural outgrowth of my hand, able to thread a pass among a bustle of moving bodies so that it arrived in a spot you didn't even know a teammate would be.

But I wanted something more from my life than basketball, so I only tried hard enough to be better than my friends, not hard enough to be the best I could be. Still, I was made captain of the team the year the coach died.

The school arranged for the players to ride to the funeral on a bus, the way we went to games. I knew that I would be expected to cry, but I also knew that would be impossible. At the service, big women hung on me, fanning me, waiting for me to fall out like the other boys, yet I couldn't will it to happen. I was sure that soon their anticipation would turn to suspicion, so I pretended I was overcome, as I had done at the funeral of the murdered children, and walked out of the church.

I knew that there was no way for me to board the bus with dry eyes, so I did again what worked before: I thought about a life without my mother. But I couldn't keep going to that same well to retrieve my tears. I needed back a bit of the faith I had lost, and with it a bit of my humanity.

I tried desperately to surrender to faith again, but it could not be done. The past year of my life disappeared into the ether as if it had never been real. It was as if it had all been a dream, a trick my mind had played on itself to stop the pain, a luscious, dreamy delusion, the kind people crave, the kind they miss when it is gone.

Just as I was reordering my own faith — falling away from it — I started to see more clearly the ways other people interpreted and interacted with the spirit world all around me — clinging to it.

There was, for instance, the exorcism that took place in the white trailer with the mint-green trim next door to Aunt Odessa's house.

A classmate of mine — a pretty, gingerbread-colored girl with big, almond-shaped eyes — lived there with her slow-talking, slow-moving grandmother. During the summers the girl's cousin often came from Dallas to visit. The cousin had short legs, a long torso, and a long face. She looked to me like a Shetland pony standing upright, though I knew that was too cruel a thing ever to say.

Something was wrong with the cousin, a little off, the way she looked at you like she was focusing on something behind you. We all figured that the something wrong was in the girl's mind, but her grandmother figured that the problem was in her soul. So the grandmother arranged to have the demon drawn out.

One evening, as dusk settled and the air cooled, a group of us teenagers milled around in the street near their trailer, swapping stories and telling jokes. An aging sedan pulled into the drive, and three big, Bible-toting women wearing long dresses and matter-of-fact expressions got out and stepped quickly into the house.

There was a silence, like the quiet before a twister sets down and tears things up. Then the chanting, praying, and singing began. Then came the loud thumps and banging. We stopped talking and started staring, listening closely to the sounds coming from the trailer. The gingerbread-colored girl came outside, embarrassed, and tried to explain what the old ladies were attempting to do. After about half an hour the cousin burst out of the door, stunned and disoriented, clothes disheveled, hair tossed. She paced around the yard like a frightened animal, breathing hard and choking back tears. We asked if she was all right, knowing full well that something was wrong. She didn't respond. After she calmed down, she went back inside. This cycle repeated itself several times over the next couple of hours. We tried to giggle away our discomfort at this thing that was happening, secretly questioning whether there might be merit in it, openly fretting over our own inaction, knowing that interfering with grandmothers and spirits was out of bounds.

Around the fringes of our tiny society, this kind of pseudo-religious, mystical fanaticism was not uncommon: the desperate and hyper-superstitious visited seers as well as preachers, sprinkled this or that around the house to ward off evil, hid a little bag or small bowls of something under a bed or in a closet to keep a wandering husband home. In their minds, the spirits, both good ones and bad ones, had to be managed. A streak of bad luck was never as simple as it seemed; something was on the move, someone had worked the roots or stirred a "haint."

Some people were thought to be witches, and others took the craft seriously.

One of our witches lived in a house across the street from the field where Papa Joe had raised the hogs, next door to the trailer where the big women had held down the frightened girl. Her name was Nellie. She was a recluse who lived with her sister in a tiny extension built on her brother's house. I often went into the main house and stared at the wall that it shared with the extension, trying to measure out Nellie and her sister's space in my mind — six feet across, I figured, not big enough for two people, not wide enough to swing a cat.

Nellie only left the house to draw water from the outside pipe, slinking around in the shadows of a large tree and darting back inside whenever someone caught sight of her. When the older sister died, Nellie was forced out into the open. She'd be seen shuffling through the streets toward town in multiple layers of moth-eaten, dark-colored clothes and a big-brimmed hat. She held her arm up over her face, the way people do when they first step from the dark into the light.

Nellie was a dark-skinned woman, but her face, at least what we could see of it, was covered in white powder, like a woman just finished making biscuits. There was a space where her eyes must have been, but the shadow from the hat fell hard there. You dared not look close enough to make out those eyes anyway. Who knew what might happen to a child who stared into the eyes of a witch.

When she passed, some children taunted her, calling her ugly, although no one ever really saw the whole of her face. In response, she hissed like a snake, scattering them like rats. I was convinced that she was a witch, but my mother was quick to set me straight: "Ain't nothin' wrong with Nellie but crazy."

Mr. Riley, who lived north of town, was different. Whereas children feared Nellie because she hid in the shadows, grown folks feared Mr. Riley because he seemed to command them. He was the conjure man who, years later, in 1994, spurred a couple of sisters from Arcadia to gouge out the eyes of a third sister, to purge her of a demon.

The woman who lost her eyes, a second-grade schoolteacher, had gone to Mr. Riley complaining of headaches. He told her that she was under attack from a demon. So the woman's sisters loaded her and their children into a car and headed west on Interstate 20, toward Dallas. The women ditched the car they were in, because they thought it was possessed, and rented a new one. They left their children with strangers at a house with a cross out front. And in a house outside Dallas that doubled as a church they beat the sister and tried to press garlic into her eyes before gouging them out, authorities believed with their bare hands. On national television, on *The Phil Donahue Show,* the eyeless woman defended her zealous sisters — better to live in darkness than be condemned to hell.

My mother didn't believe in consulting seers enough to try it, but she wasn't enough of a doubter to flout it. She constantly reminded us, only half jokingly, not to let anybody "feed us granddaddy legs," which she thought a common hex. Voodoo was beyond the pale, but superstition was doctrine. My mother held to an elaborate code of superstitions that she had adopted from Mam' Grace:

If your left hand itched, you were getting a letter. If your right one itched, you were getting money. If someone swept your feet with a broom, you were going to jail. If a dog howled, someone was going to die. If you dreamed of fish, someone was going to have a baby. It was bad luck if you broke a mirror, had a black cat cross in front of you, or traveled with raw peanuts. And if you threw peanut hulls around the back door, your parents were going to argue.

My mother never arched her eyebrows, because Mam' Grace had told her that a woman once did so and went blind. She never started anything on a Friday that she couldn't finish in a day, because Mam' Grace had told her that a lady once started a dress for her little girl on a Friday but didn't finish. The little girl died that night, and the lady had to bury her in the dress.

Whatever she'd heard Mam' Grace say was gospel to my mother. I had come to believe that, in many ways, my mother viewed Mam' Grace as her real mother. That's why she had run from the house when Mam' Grace died. That's why the tears had flowed out of her as they never would again. Mam' Grace, the woman who had drifted like a raft through the Valley of the Shadow, was more her mother than Big Mama, the woman who had floated from husband to husband until she found the ocean.

Everyone around me seemed to be running scared from a spirit, and it all began to look iffy to me. My faith was slowly eroding. Religion itself increasingly seemed a hollow homage to an eviscerated idea, a thing done out of the momentum of its always having been done.

Finally I fell back on the original God of life, the God that exists apart from books and rules and fear, the God that we first come to know before we know much of anything, God as only children know God.

Children see God every day; they just don't call it that. It's the summer sky painted with cumulus clouds by day and sequined with a million stars by night. It's the sweet whispers of sweet gum trees and the sounds riding the tops of honeysuckle-scented breezes. Children feel God stuffed into brown fluffy dogs with stitches strong enough to withstand a good squeeze, and on the lips of round women who can't get enough sugar from Chocolate.

I began to believe that God is us and nature, beauty and love, mystery and majesty, everything right and good. But I kept my new beliefs to myself, knowing that I had earned myself a new label, one just as bad as the other two, one anathema to all I'd ever known: not only punk and nigger, but now backslider.

That didn't mean that I wouldn't spend much of my life chasing the feeling of being "saved" the way it was written and relayed, the way that I had felt it, for the high of it, that feeling of floating through air. I would. I would conscientiously try to trick myself into returning to that place — to relive the remarkable, incomparable peace I had gotten from it. But it was hopeless. It could not be done. Once the curtain has been pulled back, the wizard as you knew him can never be real again.

7

Another Boy's Baby

I'm pregnant." Those are the two words that changed my life, again.

I was a senior in high school. I hadn't had a real girlfriend since I shared Jesus with the cheerleader. That courtship ended when I moved away from religion and she moved away from town.

With no new girl to fixate on, I turned my attention to maintaining the person I had become while paying respect to the person I used to be, and on pretending to be "the Big Cat" while still looking out for the underdog. I began to negotiate a fine social line, thin as a kite string, between soaring and remaining grounded, between being a popular boy and remembering that I had once felt like an invisible one.

I knew that the most fortunate kids generally steered clear of the least fortunate, but those were the ones I was drawn to.

The least fortunate were kids like the boy at school with a severe mental disability. "Retarded" was the word folks used in those days. He had unkempt hair that rose in stiff peaks like the burrs that fell from the sweet gum trees. He had eyes that looked in two directions at the same time, and he walked bent over, rising up on his toes at the end of every step, like a boy about to run. Folks said that his mother beat him so badly that he hid under the house with the dogs.

He didn't want much from me: just a high-five and a smile from the boy who played basketball, the one who never laughed at him. Whenever he saw me, he ran to me with the joyful innocence of a child, loose and happy, the way I had run across the basketball court as a small boy. After he'd slapped me high-five, he'd follow me around, a few paces back, there but not, his face looking like he wanted to say something he didn't have the words for. I knew that feeling. I knew what it felt like to want to say something but not have the words.

So I did a tiny thing by not doing another: I didn't shoo him away as others did. And I didn't let my friends make fun of him. I wanted him to know that when he was near me he'd be safe, that no one would laugh, and that he didn't have to hide with the dogs. It wasn't real bravery, just humanity.

At home, I became obsessed with the idea of taking care of things. I first tried my hand with pets. My experiences were always unfortunate. There was the black and white billicat that hid each morning beneath my bed and, as my feet searched for the floor, scratched my ankle until the blood came. There was the pink-eyed white rabbit that disappeared after tunneling its way out of the pen I built on the ground. There was the yellow and green parakeet that froze to death the first night I had it because I didn't know better than to leave its uncovered cage near our drafty window.

But children were different. I had a way with them. So I took a younger boy from down the street under my wing. He was the son of the neighborhood bootlegger, a woman who lived across the street from the wooded lot where I used to lounge on the fallen tree and listen to the standing ones. Every Sunday afternoon, when the liquor stores and juke joints shut down, her house lit up with a raucous bunch of men and a handful of women drinking hooch, playing cards, and dancing dirty.

She was a big, high-yellow woman with long, thin limbs. She had a nasal voice and a shiny pistol that she was quick to pull and willing to use. Like many of the other women in town, she had once shot her husband for cheating. He had jumped out the window, but not before she shot off half his heel. He would have to do the rest of his street running with a limp.

By now the bootlegger had gotten rid of the cheating husband and taken up with a smiling man who had the same complexion as hers but was much younger, full of himself and able to match her temper. She already had a grown daughter, but when she took up with the young man, to everyone's amazement she had another baby. He was an extremely light-skinned boy with a rakish crown of fine blond hair like a jumble of corn silk, who substituted *g*'s for *d*'s when he spoke.

Growing up as he did, he saw more than he should have, and he entertained me and my brothers with the details. He imitated people having sex. He described the way his daddy made hooch: "My gaddy take that wine, and my gaddy cook that wine." And he cursed with the ease of breathing, but not with malice. He delivered the words with a charming, innocent imprudence, unaware of his sin and therefore not guilty of it.

"Gammit!"

"God gamn!"

"You don't know me. I'll cuss yo' gamn ass out."

I did my best to be an advocate and a mentor to him, to be the kind of big brother that I wanted, to protect him from trauma as best I could, to compensate for what I had lacked.

Besides my mentoring, I still wanted to be a politician, so I started to look beyond Gibsland for ways of speaking and behaving that would shake loose the obvious signs of my strapped upbringing.

I began to emulate two men. One was the Reverend Dr. Martin Luther King, a man I looked up to the way most children looked up to athletes and movie stars. I saw in him simple pride and easy grace, a sort of righteous stoicism — stiff-backed and forward-facing, with a quiet resolve born of long suffering.

For more polish, I looked to the images of a man being beamed into our house from across the ocean, to a prince, the one who a few years before had married a bashful-looking woman named Diana. He was my namesake, Charles. Prince Charles — I liked the ring of that. I pictured myself as a prince — not him, but like him. I studied the way he held his head — up, just so, not haughty, but apart — and the way he held his hands, clasped in front of or behind his body, or one in the pocket of a suit jacket, chest always forward. I studied the way he stood — no fidgeting and no slouching, posture like a pine tree, straight up, tall and slim, a certain coolness in the shade he threw. Thereafter, whenever I wanted to be impressive in public, I mimicked the manners of a King and a prince.

The only place this didn't work was on the basketball court. There I shed my bent toward coolness, my aversion to fighting, and became prone to aggression, a tendency that spread to my teammates. We became involved in so many fights and near fights in my senior year that the district warned that one more flare-up would get us banned from the state playoffs. Other teams were aware of our warning and would taunt us and pick on me, in particular, because I was proving to be among the most explosive. I barely understood where the anger came from, only that it was there, pouring out with the sweat.

That year, our school arranged to play the team of the academy where many of the white children from our town went to school. When I walked into the gym that night I knew the game was about more than basketball. The bleachers were completely filled — white people on one side and black people on the other. There was an odd energy in the air that heightened the intensity of both teams. With every blocked shot or three-pointer, the whites or the blacks stood and cheered, each reaction outsized.

As the game drew to an end, we held a slim lead. Our new coach told my teammates to get the ball to me so that I could run out the clock. But two of the white boys trapped me against the baseline, and another came over and started to slap my arms and shoulders behind the shield of his teammates — not trying to take the ball, but attempting, I was sure, to make me react violently and kill our playoff chances.

He got his wish. I erupted in anger, lunging for him. My teammates ran to restrain me: "Don't do it, Blow, you know what they're tryin' to do." I saw that everyone in the gym had risen to their feet, tense and scowling, ready to explode. I realized that if I swung at the boy, not only would our playoff dreams be dashed, but I might destroy the fragile truce black and white folks had maintained in Gibsland for a century. I had to learn to be as controlled on the court as off it.

My efforts to transform myself in all ways were going well until I fell for a girl in my class named Evelyn. She, her brother, and a girl cousin had moved from Texas the year before to live with their grandmother in Gibsland. This was not uncommon. Hometown folks who'd moved away and had children who got out of control in the cities often sent them home to Gibsland.

Evelyn had a short, sassy haircut — rows of curls on the sides and back no bigger than the round of a Magic Marker, and a lick of hair pushed up at the forehead. She had a pretty smile with wet, pomegranate-colored lips, and a laugh so light and sweet that it rained down happiness on all of us like a sprinkle of powdered sugar.

She was a popular girl and a talented basketball player, launching soft, left-handed shots from beyond the three-point line, shots that almost always seemed to fall into the basket. Everything about her said "cool." Maybe that's why she walked with her chin held high — not arrogant, but confident. Cool.

Her boyfriend had been a boy named Baron, who was a year older than us and had been on the basketball team with me. He was being raised by his mother; his father was in jail for beating a man to death. At the start of our senior year, after Baron graduated, he too went to jail for killing a man. Soon after, Evelyn made clear that I was the new target of her affections.

It seemed odd, but I didn't question it. Boys hijacked by hormones don't really think, they chase. They see risk and consequences as if through the wrong end of a telescope: smaller and pushed far away. There was no way for me to resist the lure of pomegranate lips and chocolate thighs, no way to turn back when clumsy advances were met with such warm agreement. This was the kind of feeling that the male figures who came in the night did not bring, the burning beneath the breastbone, the kind of heat that blinds a boy and reduces reason to ashes.

Evelyn spent many of her afternoons at the house of her aunt, a West End woman not much older than us, who tried too hard to be our friend and not hard enough to be grown. She was the kind of woman who would neither tell her age nor act it. The aunt's house was near my house, just beyond a bend in the highway from the upholstery shop. Evelyn's cousin liked Alphonso, my friend who looked at other boys with the kind of look that made them beat themselves up, and whom girls now looked at like they were dreaming. So every afternoon after school, Alphonso and I walked to the aunt's house to meet the girls.

The aunt entertained us with profane stories about loose living and ghetto loving, talking more to Evelyn and her cousin than to me and Alphonso, teaching them how to milk the most out of a man, and the limits of such tactics. One day when we were there, she warned the girls, "Don't neva let yo' ol' man buy all yo' stuff, 'cause when he leave, he gone want it all back. I was messing with this ol' man one time and we went out to eat. We got ta arg'ing and he said, 'Gimme back all my shit!' I got to thanking, 'Dis his dress, dese his shoes, dese his draws, dis his damned wig.' Hell, if I had-a gave him back all his shit, I woulda walked outta there butt nekked and ball-headed."

One day when the aunt was out, Evelyn led me to a bedroom. No words passed between us, but none were needed. She was inviting me to have sex. She took off her clothes and lay back on the bed. I took off mine and lay on top of her. I didn't have a condom. I had never needed one. And she didn't request that I wear one. I didn't ask if she was on the pill. She didn't volunteer the information. None of those thoughts ever occurred to me.

My body entered hers and my senses caught fire. The world slowed down and my mind sped up. My body felt stiff and numb. Her body felt wet and soft and warm, the kind of warmth that piqued the nerves with the crisp of coldness, like summer rain falling on bare shoulders or creek water running over bare feet.

Soon we melted into each other and collapsed in exhaustion. The deed had been gladly done, the pact of passion sealed. We rose and dressed ourselves in silence the way too-young people do, not having the words to express love or gratitude or concern, unable to find a graceful way to part ways.

A few weeks later, she told me: "I'm pregnant." I was stunned. I didn't ask if I was the father, I simply assumed that I was, and she said nothing to confirm or deny my assumption. In that moment the whole of my life had to be redrawn. "Father" had to be fit into it. I got up the nerve to tell my mother. "Evelyn is pregnant." She responded with one line: "Is it yours?" "Yes," I said, although I realized then that I hadn't actually asked. My mother simply walked to her room and closed the door.

I don't remember much about my relationship with Evelyn after that, only that we soon broke up. But I do remember thinking constantly about how best to do right by the baby once it came.

I remember the day Evelyn's brother came to my class, asked to see me, and told me that she had had the baby. A little girl, to whom Evelyn gave the name I'd suggested. Happy, I ran to my mother's classroom to share the news. My mother didn't have a class that period, so she was tidying up. I swung open the door and said with a smile, "Evelyn had the baby." My mother responded, without ever stopping her tidying, "You know that's not your baby, right?" I didn't respond. I just walked out. My heart wouldn't let me hear it. I wrote off my mother's comment as derision born of disappointment.

The first time I held the baby my heart melted: her writhing and cooing in the cradle of my arms, my knees weak and trembling, my elbows locked for fear that I might drop her. I fell instantly into the deepest, most primal kind of love, the kind that makes a man willing to lay down his life or work himself to death. She was tiny and light and precious. Beautiful. And she smelled sweet, intoxicating even. But it was her innocence that moved me most: glassy eyes that had never seen death, soft feet that had never fled from fear, delicate hands that had never thumbed a Bible to hover a finger above the word "abomination."

In mid-May, just before graduation, I flew to Knoxville, Tennessee. I had won my way to the international science fair, held there that year. I was trying to keep myself focused on my studies, to find a balance between being a good father and being a good student.

My science fair project was about why the so-called Star Wars anti–ballistic missile system, proposed by President Reagan, wouldn't succeed. I built a big wooden board with an inserted section for a diorama of the earth and the sky to illustrate how the system was supposed to work, and made cutouts for a television and a VCR so that I could play a videotape of a documentary I had recorded showing why it wouldn't work. It looked impressive, but I had violated one of the basic rules of science fair projects: I hadn't actually done an experiment. My project was basically a research project. Still, I'd won the district fair.

I wanted to be impressive at the international science fair, so in the weeks leading up to it I went to the parish library and checked out every etiquette book I could find. I read those books front to back. I felt I had uncovered a trove of secrets that had been withheld from me.

The flight to Knoxville was my first time in an airplane. I saw the world from above, the way God saw it: dotted with ponds and crossed by rivers. In spots it looked to me like the quilts Mama and Big Mama made — parcels of tan, khaki, and ecru; lime, emerald, and kelly green; squares, rectangles, and trapezoids. I drew comfort from that thought as turbulence jostled the plane, and I resisted the urge to throw up.

I arrived in Knoxville, but my project did not. The airline said they'd lost it. I suspected that, being heavy and wooden as it was, the thing had in fact been mishandled, probably badly damaged, and they were simply covering it up. While all the other students stood proudly before their projects in the large convention hall, I would stand before an empty space where my project should have been, explaining to the baffled judges that it had been "lost" in transit.

At the first dinner in Knoxville, I sat at a table with some other students. As I silently reveled in the fact that I now knew what all the spoons and forks were for and what to do if food fell on the floor, an older man approached and asked if a vacant seat was taken. It wasn't, so he sat. He was a distinguished-looking man with kind eyes. He was very polite and engaging, asking each of us about our projects, commenting on each one as if he were truly interested.

He said that he had been one of the scientists on the Manhattan Project, information he relayed with the kind of pride that's saddled with sadness. I didn't know what it was until he explained it, but I knew from the way he had said the words — Manhattan Project — that it weighed on him, and that he was conflicted about his role in it.

The juxtaposition of this dinner with the rest of my life was striking. Just days before, I had been in our living room with Paul, trying to explain to him that the cartoon characters on television that flummoxed him so were not people dressed up in costumes but thousands of drawings. I had gone from talking to a man who didn't understand, nor had ever seen, the world, to sitting with a man who had helped make a weapon that could destroy it.

The next day, I realized that one of the Westinghouse Science Talent Search winners was around the corner from my position in the exhibition hall. He had also done a project on the Star Wars program, although his seemed to be a rigorous computer simulation of the laser system. I walked past, scoping it out from afar, as if sizing up all the competition on the row. I was in awe, and I shrank with embarrassment, tucking my head into my shoulders the way Uncle Paul often did. The boy's board was extraordinarily tall and covered in theories and mathematical equations that I couldn't make heads or tails of—hieroglyphs to me. I stared at the marks the way Uncle Paul stared at the cartoons—flummoxed. The boy stood before the board, modest, bookish, and confident. I knew then that the competition in life was not at home, not in a little segregated town divided by a shallow ditch. This was the competition—the bookish boy and his extra-tall board.

I told myself that I would never underestimate the competition again, now that I had gotten a gander at it. No one would cut me slack because I was a small-town boy. No one would show pity because I had messed up and made a baby. I would have to rise above.

I got back to Gibsland on a Saturday. Graduation was that Sunday. I walked across the stage several times, not only accepting my diploma but being honored as valedictorian and receiving several scholarships.

The week after graduation, I was visiting Evelyn and the baby at her grandmother's apartment when my cousin Faith, who was a friend of Evelyn's, came to visit. Papa Joe was also Faith's great-grandfather, because Papa Joe had stepped out on Mam' Grace and had a child in sin. Faith and I were not close, but we tolerated each other.

That day, she walked into the apartment, spoke to us all, and then asked to hold the baby. Then she said the words that snapped the sense back into me: "Charles, she don't look nothin' like you." Maybe she was saying it to be mean, or maybe she was trying to awaken a cousin without losing a friend. Whatever the reason, she was right. The child bore absolutely no resemblance to me and only a passing resemblance to Evelyn. For some reason, I hadn't allowed myself to notice that before.

My eyes went glassy like the baby's, like I was seeing things for the first time.

Slowly, the uneasy feeling settled over me that I had been holding another boy's baby. I had quieted the voices in my head that condemned me for my carelessness and resigned myself to fatherhood. A part of me had gotten used to the idea, comfortable with it. Part of me desperately wanted the baby to be mine, but in my heart, in that moment, I no longer believed she was.

For my science project I had counted the ways the multibillion-dollar Star Wars program wouldn't work, but I had never allowed myself to count the months of Evelyn's supposed gestation — six, maybe seven, from that time we'd had sex, not nine. And I had never allowed myself to question why Evelyn had swung so quickly from Baron to me — from a boy who had gone to prison to one who was going to college.

I could taste the acid on the back of my tongue like I was about to vomit, the lies she had fed me wanting to come back up.

I don't know if Evelyn saw the truth settle over me that day Faith made her remark, but the next week she moved away with the baby. No notice. No new address. No phone number. Just gone. I never heard from her again.

After she left, people talked openly about how it had been Baron's baby, not mine, and I felt like a fool. I thought I knew the pain of betrayal through and through, but in a way this deception was even more hurtful than the others. How exactly is a boy supposed to fall out of the deepest love he's ever known with the most beautiful thing he's ever seen?

I would never know what caused Evelyn to devise her plan or to abandon it, or even be absolutely sure that I was right and she had done wrong. All I knew was that in my heart, in my bones, I no longer believed. I figured that she had probably placed a safe bet after a bad one, and maybe after the fact she had thought better of it.

Whatever her reason, and whatever the truth, I now had another hole in my heart.

8

The Brothers

I didn't go away to college as much as I ran away to it.

I needed to go somewhere not haunted by memories. I needed to find a place where no one had ever died — no old woman surrendering her life as a last act of beauty; no old man with syrup-colored eyes coughing up lots of blood; no dead children at the bottom of a pond. I needed a place where there had never been a betrayal — no one whispering, "It's just a game"; no hand moving like a snake; no trapped girl whose laugh rained down like sugar and whose lies rose up like bile.

My dream of escape had centered on up north. Down south was too close for a boy who needed to run away. For no reason in particular, I had set my eyes on William and Mary, although being as it was in Virginia, it was still technically in the South. Maybe I would make it in, and maybe they would give me a basketball scholarship. But I never actually applied. In my heart I was convinced that I had no chance, that I was dreaming beyond my talents. Besides, my mother didn't want me to go anywhere far, and couldn't have paid for it if I did. But if I couldn't escape north, I would escape farther south. I applied to

Louisiana State University, in Baton Rouge. And because I was the valedictorian of my class, I was guaranteed a full scholarship. I decided to take it.

But from the beginning, my mother raised doubts and built an argument designed to keep me closer. She was scared and nervous for me. She still saw me as her baby, certainly not a man, and couldn't imagine not being able to get to me if I needed her. But I was determined to go.

That is, until the recruiter at Grambling called me to his office to review the details of a scholarship his school would offer me.

Grambling State University was the black school in the region that had supplanted Gibsland's Coleman College. It was the place where my mother had gone to learn to make things like the stuffed dog with the button eyes and to get her teaching certification; where Nathan had gone and met the roommate who looked at me like he was sucking candy; and where my brothers William and Robert, like most Gibsland students, went by default.

Still, I had never considered going to college there. In fact, I was hostile to the idea. It was too close for a boy who needed to run away.

Grambling had its share of smart kids and passionate professors, but with its "Where Everybody Is Somebody" motto and redemption sensibility, it also drew and admitted many otherwise unadmittable students, young people in need of a second chance and a fresh start. Many of them were from rough parts of big cities — refugees from urban warfare and bad schools, in search of a safe place. At Grambling they didn't have to worry about what color they wore, about whose turf they were on, about catching a stray bullet shot wild and loose from a passing car. They could just breathe — thick, pine-scented air under big empty skies. They could read and learn, party and make friends, grow and become something. "Somebody."

At our meeting, the recruiter — a white man — gave me the "Your People Need You" talk, which sounded a little odd coming from him. "LSU doesn't *need* you! Louisiana Tech doesn't *need* you! Grambling *needs* you!" And, at the time, I still believed that the baby needed me. So, after some deliberation, I submitted and accepted the call. I would go to Grambling and stay close to Gibsland.

I went to college before most other freshmen arrived, enrolling for the summer session that began in June. I declared a double major, in English — because I liked writing — and prelaw — because I figured being a lawyer would be the best route to becoming a politician. I took three classes that summer and got one of the most coveted work-study positions on campus — in the admissions office — because one of the women who worked there had grown up down the street from the House with No Steps. Like everyone else on that street, she even now called me Char'esBaby.

There were a few other students working in the office, including a boy named Al-David, though folks called him Chopper for some reason that I couldn't figure. He was a golden boy — in both color and concept — whose hair was a surfeit of soft waves and whose eyes were those of a person the world had treated kindly. But there was something about him — in the smile that didn't quite stretch to its full width or the gaze that stayed locked on you one beat too long — that hinted at a cruel streak.

The admissions office was in Adams Hall, the president's building. Unbeknownst to me, this was where the cool local kids worked. Outwardly, I was a high-performing hick with a self-possessed manner — an underdog they didn't mind rooting for. Inside was hiding the boy who dug "treasure" from junkyards, ate dirt, and was shadowed by betrayal.

Often, without being fully aware of it, I withdrew into myself, silence falling over me like the dark on a moonless night. Some folks read that silence as burgeoning conceit. I found this curious. I also realized that their misreading did the same thing to them that Alphonso's looks had done to folks in elementary school: it caused them to search themselves for flaws because they assumed that's what I was doing. In this way, a quirk became an armament. I began to pretend that these silent spells were purposeful.

And I began to suffer a common social climber's delusion: feeling that I was from poverty but not of it, that I had been born out of sorts with my ambitions, that my struggle to correct the imbalance was a righteous pursuit — that I was not moving out of my element, but into it.

Chopper and I spent the days cracking jokes and talking basketball and getting food. He wasn't just cool, he was smart. Exceedingly smart. Brilliant even. With him I enjoyed the experience of not only matching wits but being outwitted.

All I knew of Chopper outside the admissions office was that he was the older brother of a Grambling High School point guard I'd considered a rival — a boy named Brandon — and that he dated one of the most beautiful girls on campus. And that he was a member of one of the school's four fraternities — the one everyone called the "Pretty Boys" because they seemed to attract and admit candidates who were boy-band handsome, the ones who dressed well and moved smoothly, the ones girls cooed over. The other fraternities hewed to similarly simplistic stereotypes: rowdy boys, nerdy boys, or country boys.

Near the end of the summer session, I came to understand the racial undertones of what the white recruiter had told me to secure my commitment. Conversations about history, race, equality, and justice with Grambling teachers and students lit a fire in me and helped to mold my view of myself while allowing me to bend the views of other students. I believed then that not only did Grambling need me, but I needed Grambling.

When the fall semester began, the campus was flooded with students, nearly half of them — three thousand — freshmen, many of whom would drop out before the next year. I had graduated in a class of about thirty students, and soon realized that at Grambling I was going to be just one of many, a status change I refused to accept. I couldn't go back to being barely visible. So I decided to do one of the things I had always done to stand out: I would run for class president.

The problem was that I didn't have much money to finance the campaign. So I put on my only suit and went to the only bank in Gibsland and asked to speak to the president. After waiting a few minutes, his secretary waved me in. I told him what I wanted to do and that I needed help financing it. He smiled politely and nodded, saying he was proud that a local boy would have such an ambition and the gumption to ask him for a campaign contribution. He had one of the tellers give me a few hundred dollars and wished me well.

I used some of the money to buy plywood and paint, to make billboards to place around campus. With the rest I made flyers and cards. I adopted the design from my favorite T-shirt, one with Martin Luther King on it, replacing his image with mine.

A friend from Gibsland, who had been a trainer on my high school basketball team, helped me put the flyers everywhere we could think of. We slid one under every door in the freshman dorms, stuck one on every mirror in the bathrooms, and taped one inside every bathroom stall at eye level. Every evening I went to a wall on the side of the cafeteria always lined with freshmen. I would start at one end of the line and introduce myself to every person, asking for their vote, working my way to the other end.

Some laughed at my cheap suit, the one I kept remixing all week with different shirts and ties: "Is that polyester?" Some teased me about the flyers in the bathroom: "Dude, I can't even take a dump without seeing yo' damned face." Some tired of my persistence: "I already *got* a flyer." But most admired me for trying hard and continuing to smile regardless of what they said.

When election day came, I won by a landslide.

Moments after the results were announced, a sports car pulled up and Miss Grambling stepped out. She was the college queen, elected the previous spring. Her name was Jackie, and she happened to be the daughter of the president of the school.

She was strikingly beautiful — flawless brown skin, fine sandy hair arranged in a rising crown of curls, a natural dark smokiness around her eyes that other girls tried to create with makeup. She congratulated me and told me that I needed to hurry to a department store in the town of Ruston, three miles east of Grambling, to be measured for suits that she had chosen for the four class presidents to wear.

One of the most public functions of each class president was to escort his class queen to football games as part of Miss Grambling's court. Her escort was traditionally the Student Government Association president, but this year that president was a girl, so both girls were escorted by their boyfriends.

The football stadium was named for the head coach, Eddie Robinson, who a few years before had become the winningest coach in college football history. It was a sunken stadium, carved out of the top of a hill, with sounds flowing up and over the rim — the crunch of shoulders, the roar of fans, the funky rhythms of Grambling's famous marching band — like lava from the caldera of a volcano.

In front of the band, in the first row, were the Orchesis dancers: girls in sequined leotards and heeled pumps sashaying a fusion of jazz, modern, and dirty dance.

The crowd roared, waving streamers and banners, chanting to the tune of the band:

> G S . . . G S . . . G S . . . G S . . . U,
> (Pause)
> I thought you knew!

The fans of the visiting team often joined in, but with a slight twist. They filled in our pause with a purple phrase:

G S ... G S ... G S ... G S ... U,
(AIN'T SHIT!)
I thought you knew!

And back and forth it went from us to them.

Miss Grambling's court made its entrance midway through the first quarter and slowly walked in descending class order, presidents and queens locking arms, down the stadium stairs to the front row.

At halftime, after the band had performed, we walked once around the field and up to the president's skybox on the other side of the stadium. There we were introduced to notable alumni, wealthy donors, and the occasional visiting celebrity. Our job was to be gracious and to represent the best of the Grambling student — popular boys and pretty girls, all smart — to loosen donors' pockets.

From the first time I met the other three class presidents, they could talk about only one thing: they all wanted to pledge the Pretty Boys' fraternity. I didn't really know what it meant to pledge a fraternity, and I had no desire to join a secret society, living as I did a secret solitude. But I soon got caught up in their enthusiasm. They made it clear that boys in fraternities — and those who wanted to be — dismissed people who didn't want to pledge as GDIs, goddamned independents.

The presidents also pointed out that every twentieth-century black man worth his salt had belonged to one of the four black fraternities on campus: Thurgood Marshall, Frederick Douglass, W.E.B. Du Bois, and Martin Luther King. George Washington Carver, Ralph Abernathy, Jesse Jackson, and Huey P. Newton. Benjamin Mays, Percy Sutton, and Johnnie Cochran. James Weldon Johnson and Langston Hughes. Michael Jordan. Everyone.

At Grambling the Pretty Boys ruled, they said. It was Chopper's fraternity as well as the university president's.

There were two kinds of boys who wanted to be Pretty Boys, those seeking to enshrine their swagger and those seeking to compensate for their lack of it.

The class presidents lacked it. And they were so obsessed with the notion of inclusion-as-completion that they couldn't see that it was their thirst that undid them. Still, they spoke of it the way infertile couples speak of babies: beaming with hope but pregnant with disappointment, yearning for something that was not to be.

The Pretty Boys were supposed to be ladies' men — like Chopper. The presidents weren't. They were all short and wonky, and none of the three had a girlfriend as best I could tell. They were about as different from Chopper as boys could be, the kind of boys I would have steered clear of if the choice were mine.

But their excitement was contagious. Furthermore, the other presidents told me that the Pretty Boys' motto was "Achievement in Every Field of Human Endeavor," and that appealed to me. If wanting to be in that fraternity was good enough for all of them, and for Chopper, I figured it was good enough for me.

I believed, too, that I had advantages that the other presidents didn't. I wasn't a pretty boy, or ladies' man either, but I was tall and had been a high school basketball star. In male culture that carried weight. And, since back in grade school, when Russell had anointed me and Alphonso accepted me, I had been one of the popular boys. I knew how that world worked — what popular people thought about and worried about, what they valued and what they feared. I also had artistic skills the fraternity could use. And I knew Chopper, whom the members of the fraternity lionized.

The class presidents told me that the only way to "make line," to become a member of the pledge group, was to visit each of the members, "the Brothers," at their homes and to lobby them for their votes. In fact, they had notebooks with all the Brothers' names and addresses and a tally of how often they had visited each one.

I told them that the next time they visited someone, I wanted to go. With the other presidents I visited all the Brothers, most several times, except the one I refused to visit, Nash, a square boy with a thick neck and bushy brows that sat like two rolls of quarters over hazel-green eyes. They were the kind of eyes that stirred up fear in folks. He was all muscle and anger and trouble. Nash didn't fit the Pretty Boy image.

He was also the fraternity's most notorious hazer, known for pad-dling prospective pledges as a prerequisite for his advocacy and his vote. I was adamant that I would not be hazed before I was sure I had made the pledge group. In truth, I was still trying to reconcile myself to the idea of being hazed at all. It seemed such a foreign concept — sub-mitting oneself to beatings by boys who would call you brother.

I wanted to push the thought of it as far off as possible.

The first semester, to save money, I lived off campus in a rented trailer with my brother Robert. But for the spring semester I decided to live on campus, for two reasons. First, if I made line, I didn't want any of the Brothers coming to the trailer during pledging and bothering Rob-ert; and second, because many of the freshmen felt that the president of the class should live on campus like most other freshmen.

Because of my grades and my scholarship, I qualified for housing in the honors dorm, but I turned it down. I told the housing office to put me in the freshman dorm: if the freshmen wanted me to live on campus, I was going to live with them. It was the worst dorm on cam-pus, Pinchback Hall, named for the man who during Reconstruction became the first and only black governor of Louisiana. Perfect for me, the boy who wanted to be the next one.

But someone in the housing office had an odd sense of humor.

On move-in day, I walked into my assigned room. It was dark and filled with the acrid odor of an unwashed body and unwashed clothes. Before me was a boy: shiny and dark and covered by rivulets of raised veins. His shirtless body cut a silhouette against the light of the small window behind him. As my eyes adjusted to the darkness, I could make out the contours of his face. It had the serious look of someone whom joy had abandoned and trouble found. Like Chester, but without the smile.

He introduced himself, "Pookie," as we appraised each other. Neither of us spoke, but physiognomic judgments passed between us, embedded in glares of disapproval. His judgment of me: sweet. Mine of him: bitter. Without prompting, he began to tell his story. He had recently been released from prison. He said that his mother, who worked in the district attorney's office in his hometown, was the person who had him put away.

The way he told the story was not the way you talk to make a friend but rather to mark a space. He wanted to register the room as his, the way a dog pisses on a post or growls a lesser dog away from a bone. It didn't work, but I recognized the effort and resented it. It was a form of aggression, and I didn't knuckle under to aggression. I was thin, but I wasn't weak.

We were as different as two people could be. I could have stayed in the room and battled with him for dominance, but that seemed a waste of time and energy. I was the freshman class president trying to make a pledge line. So I went back to the housing office and demanded a room change.

They switched me to a room with a brawny Cajun boy who liked to cook rice and beans on a hot plate. He was easygoing and kept to himself, staying out of my way as I stayed out of his. Still, every time Pookie saw me on campus, he'd yell "Roommate!" in a sardonic tone. It seemed to be his way of never letting me forget what he thought he'd done: scared me off.

That semester, I took a freshman writing class, one with a couple of hundred students. One of our assignments was to write a personal essay. The day before the assignment was due, still uninspired, I stayed up all night, drinking Dr Pepper, taking NoDoz, and writing on my electric typewriter about the only thing I could think to write: the day

I was baptized. As the sun rose and time for class approached, I was just finishing. I snatched the last page out of the typewriter and dashed off to class. I turned in the assignment without ever reading it over, just hoping that I wouldn't fail.

In a couple of weeks the professor had graded all the papers. In class he said, "One of these essays really stood out, so I thought I'd take this class period to read it to you." I was barely paying attention until he began to read. Then I perked up. He was reading my essay. The class, seemingly rapt, listened until he was done, then burst into applause. I was bursting with pride.

The professor returned everyone's essay but mine, then asked me to meet him in his office after class. There he asked, "What's your major?" I told him that I had a double major in English and prelaw and planned to go to law school. He prodded, "So, what are you going to do with an English major if you don't go to law school? Teach?" He said it like a man unhappy with his job. I didn't have an answer, but I knew I didn't want to be a teacher. He said, "Why don't you double major in mass communications and prelaw? Journalism and English are not that different. And that way, if you don't go to law school, at least you'll have a profession you'll like."

His reasoning made sense to me. The love of newspapers I'd absorbed from my mother was reinforced in high school when our 4-H Club adviser took us to visit the offices of the *Bienville Democrat* — the parish newspaper published in nearby Arcadia — and we got to typeset and print our names on actual newsprint. I wrote for the high school paper and even sent letters to the editor at the *Shreveport Times,* one of which they published — my first foray into opinion journalism. Writing and newspapers were a natural part of me, so I switched majors. I also joined the college newspaper, the *Gramblinite.*

It was a good thing I'd settled my major, because soon afterward I'd be concentrating on only one thing. The Brothers voted, and I made the pledge group — with Chopper's endorsement and over Nash's objection—along with sixteen other boys. None of them were the other presidents.

The night the Brothers let the boys know they had made the line and rounded everyone up, I was nowhere to be found. That's because I was an hour away, on a stage in Shreveport, in a military jacket and tights, performing with the Dance Theater of Harlem.

I got roped into the performance by Grambling's dance troupe instructor, a nice woman who was an alumna of the Alvin Ailey dance company. She asked me for a favor: the Dance Theater of Harlem wanted her to provide four soldiers for their Shreveport production, and she thought of me. It was nothing, really, she said: just march onto the stage at the end of the show and wave some flags. It seemed simple enough, and I wanted to help her out, so I agreed.

I thought that the dancers would all be women, but about a third of them were men—the kind of men whose company I had spent years trying not to keep. Different. Apart. But these men didn't look like the men I knew—either strong and stiff or thin and wispy. Their legs were thick like those of horses, but moved lightly like those of deer.

The night the Brothers rounded up the pledges was the night of the show. The contrast between what I was doing on that stage and what I was supposed to be doing back at school could not have been more stark. While I was in Shreveport lining up with preternaturally sculpted male dancers, the other pledges were being lined up behind a Grambling church among yelling Brothers.

When I made it back to campus late that night, someone told me in a solemn voice that I had made line and that we were to meet the next day at the apartment of the dean of pledges. I was both excited and petrified. I told no one where I'd been the night before, knowing my participation in the dance performance would have been a deal breaker among the Brothers.

We gathered at the house of Marcus G., our dean of pledges—or DP, as everyone called it—who was also the older brother of one of the boys on the line. His friends called him Kaboom because he said he had once fallen out of bed and, because he was so big, made that sound when he hit the floor: *Kaboom!*

He looked slightly agitated that night our pledge group first met at his house. He was eager to introduce us to our new reality as pledges, but also was clearly in control. He arranged us in a line from shortest to tallest and assigned us corresponding line numbers. Mine was 13, the unluckiest one. We stood in that line, wrapping around the tiny living room, wide-eyed, like the deer in the House of the Drowned Children, silent and pensive, as Kaboom came and went through the front door. On his second entry we failed to greet him, since we didn't know we were supposed to *every time*. It was just the trigger he needed for our first beating.

One of the Brothers in the room turned up the music to mask the sound of what was to come. Ironically, the song was a single from a collection of rap hits, part of KRS-One's Stop the Violence movement:

Self-Destruction, ya headed for Self-Destruction
Self-Destruction, ya headed for Self-Destruction

The irony of the song's message in light of what they were doing was lost on the Brothers, who simply liked repeating the hook.

One by one they called us to the center of the room.

"Get in the cut, muthafucka . . . and hold ya nuts!"

Almost all the other pledges had been paddled before making line, so they knew what this meant. I didn't. It meant the pledge was to get into a baseball catcher's position, with his ass held a little higher, clutching his nuts with both hands, presumably for protection against the blow. That position was called "the cut." Kaboom drew the short wooden paddle back with both hands and swung it with all his might, delivering a nerve-shattering crack to the butt.

THWOP! The unmistakable sound of wood on jeans on flesh.

The pledge said what we had been told to say: "Thanks, Big Brother! May I have another?!"

The other Brothers in the room jumped like excited animals, yelling and screaming, creating a chaotic feedback loop of alcohol and adrenaline.

"Whew! Damn! That's what I'm talkin' 'bout!"

"Y'all thought this shit was a game. This ain't no game, muthafuckas! This ain't no fuckin' Spike Lee *School Daze*. This shit is fa real! Somebody gone quit tonight. Somebody gone drop!"

And on and on it went. *THWOP! THWOP! THWOP!* "Next!" *THWOP! THWOP! THWOP!*

"Come on, muthafucka!"

I stood there thinking how bizarre and nonsensical it all seemed. Why did they need to hit us? Why were we allowing it? But I knew it was tradition. The Brothers had all been hazed as pledges, as had been the Brothers who hazed them. The logic was simple: the individual had to be broken so that the unit could be built. *E pluribus unum*: Out of many, one. It was profound but sophistic, wrong all dressed up as right. This had gone on for decades, and the Brothers must have felt they were doing what they were supposed to do, for the better of the bond.

Fraternal devotion ran deep. Some Brothers even made fraternity symbols out of wire hangers, heated them on a stove, branded them onto each other's arms, and proudly wore the puffy keloid scars that resulted.

And, as had already been drilled into us pledges, no one had ever quit — "dropped line," as it was called — and survived the ridicule of having done so. Line droppers where the lowest of the low, cowards, boys who could never live down the shame of it.

Soon it was my turn. So I did what was expected of me, against all my better judgment and good sense: I got into the cut. I stared straight ahead. I tried to brace myself for it, but nothing could have prepared me.

THWOP!

The force of the impact nearly knocked me over. I rose on my toes to keep from falling forward. The pain of it crackled through my body. My vision blurred. The sound in the room grew muted, like things had sounded underwater in the baptismal pool when I fought against the preacher. My ass and my temples began to throb. My nostrils flared, my body demanding more air than I could give it. I was on fire.

My nose was about to run, my eyes were watering despite my best efforts to prevent it, and beads of sweat were forming on my forehead. All of my instincts said, "Scream, run, cry." But I knew I couldn't. I stood firm.

"Thanks, Big Brother! May I have another?!"

There was a strange resonance for me between the hazing and Chester's betrayal: me again receiving secret abuse because I had been chosen. Only this time it wasn't sexual, and I wasn't alone. While pledging I would often recall one of my mother's sayings: You could stay in hell for a little while if you knew that you were going to get out.

As I received the blows — "bringing wood" — I focused my thoughts on the woods in the lot beyond the field where I had found silent sanctuary. Like those trees, I would not be moved.

THWOP! THWOP!

The next day, we pledges all gathered in a remote corner of the library, doing homework and trying not to draw attention to ourselves. As we sat, some of the Brothers came and went. We had been given pocket-sized notebooks in which we wrote things we needed to learn — Bible verses, pledging songs, the specific greeting for each Brother, fraternity history and protocols — and in which Brothers wrote us personal messages, usually encouragements but sometimes threats. They called the notebooks our "Brains."

That day a few of the Brothers took my Brain and wrote similar messages in it: "You surprised a lot of brothers last night. Way to stay strong."

I realized that most had expected me to crack, to break, that they had made the same judgment about me that Pookie had: sweet. But they were in for a surprise. I had been fortified by trauma, the way a bone, once broken, grows back stronger than it had been. The link between me and my body had long ago been severed. No matter what they did to it, the true me was untouched. In fact, if there was a line between acting and lying, between protecting myself and betraying myself, between crafting a new me and erasing the essential one, I no longer knew where that line was.

All this was a help in doing what I had to do: get used to the beatings. Physical hazing, brutal and nearly barbaric, was a central part of pledging. Membership came at a price, one to be paid in blood and bruises. If I wanted to be in, I had to be down.

One day I parked my car on the side of the liberal arts building, trying to avoid running into any Brothers, but there was Kaboom, just inside, beyond a large window, watching me walk toward the door.

His face shifted. His brow, snarled and heavy like a big-link chain, fell. I had seen this look before. It was the look my mother had when I cut across the basketball court as a little boy, arms stretched wide, folks snickering. When I got to the door, Kaboom said in a hushed but angry tone, "Come here!," the way a person talks when he wants to yell but has to whisper, pushing out more air than sound. "If I ever catch you walking like that again, I'm gonna fuck you up!"

Walking like what? I thought. It was that thing that others could see but I couldn't.

As best I could tell, my wrists sometimes fell limp, like something wilted, and when I moved, I floated the way a cobweb dances with the air when you sweep half of it away from the wall. I discounted these as traits I must have absorbed from the old folks with whom I spent my preschool days, all crooked hands and elegant gestures. That was the only explanation my mind would accept. But mannerisms that made sense on old folks made none on young men.

To me, the way I moved was without calculation. To others, the way

I moved seemed a conscious thing, a choice, and a bad one. Because of it, they judged me the way I had judged the male dancers in Shreveport: different, apart, athletic but feminine. I hadn't given thought to floating, but I learned to give thought to stiffness, to limit the range of my motions, to imagine that my joints had bolts in them turned half a round too tight. I learned to be ever vigilant, to the point of exhaustion, monitoring small movements, things other folks never had to think about.

But the Brothers weren't the only ones concerned. So were some of my line brothers. Mardi Gras, a campus DJ, made no secret of the fact that he didn't appreciate my being put on "his line." He didn't explicitly say why, but he didn't have to. The only person who came close to saying it was a boy named Clay, whom we elected the line president. He was a handsome, broad-shouldered ex–football player whose hopes of playing college ball had been dashed in high school by a knee injury that left him with a slight limp.

One night we were all in the apartment of one of our line brothers, hiding from the Brothers and trying to learn the information in our Brains. Most of the boys were clustered in small groups, helping each other study, but I was sitting alone on the floor with my back against the wall.

Clay walked over, sat down beside me, and said: "Hey, man, I ain't gonna lie. The Brothers used to ask us who we didn't want to make line with us, and you were always on my list, but you are really being tough, and that's cool."

I knew exactly what he was saying. He too had had his suspicions about me, he too saw that thing others did but I didn't, he too thought I would be soft, only to realize that I was harder than most. Maybe I should have been offended by what he said, but I wasn't. He was the first person there who had even come close to saying to my face what I was sure many were whispering behind my back — "There's something wrong with that boy" — and I appreciated his honesty. "Thanks," I said.

What no one knew was that I had my own secret worries. I had never felt a physical attraction to my high school friends or teammates, and the idea of physical contact with another boy was still unfathomable. It was a barrier not to be crossed, like the fence at the segregated cemetery back home. Everything would say so, explicitly and not — the Bible, the old men under the shade trees, Lawrence's lifeless body tied to a strange bed, my mother's worried look, my own inhibitions. But I worried that, being in close quarters with so many pledges, boys I didn't know, my body might react against my wishes, against everything I knew and felt. Now that I was older, the male figures that once came only in the night slipped with ease into daytime thinking.

The figures were still not overtly sexual; physical contact was not the logical conclusion of what I felt, as best I could tell. What I wanted — needed — was to be chosen, constantly. It was in being desired that my own desire abided. And girls performed that function well. That was why I had been so blind to Evelyn's deception, so enthralled by her enticements: because she had chosen me.

And girls' bodies just made sense to me. They were soft, with welcoming spots and curvy places. Other. Feminine. One thing that was always clear, from the moment Chester had pushed up behind me, was that I wasn't attracted to masculinity in its physicality: muscles and gruffness and aggression. I could admire it, envy it, even want to emulate it, but I didn't desire it. In fact, being the object of aggression actually raised my ire. This ensured that I would never be attracted to my friends.

Still, I steered clear of any flirty boys, boys who took on women's ways, who I thought might be about choosing, so no mistake might be made. That was what worried me: that some smiling boy might slip past the barrier my mind had erected, and my body might react without my permission. I didn't yet know my body well enough to trust it.

Whatever I might feel about guys was subordinate and fluctuant, and I wanted to forever keep it bottled up tight, like the cork in a whiskey jug. Not even a word, lest I speak it into existence. I had come to see my silence and self-control as demonstrations of strength, a private pride and, literally, a means of survival.

In fact, action aside, my silence was giving power to angst and stealing virtue from courage. Fear had become a prison and nearly a coffin.

It was simple, but complicated.

I was no longer the child victim. I was eighteen, a young man, and with that came a new responsibility of self-acceptance and full disclosure. But, as it is for so many, that turn was hard for me to make. I didn't yet accept the fact that you couldn't be a man and be afraid, that part of growing up was speaking up, that the lamp of honesty actually shines brightest in the darkest places — in the absence of understanding and the presence of hostility.

I continued to hold out hope that I could rid myself of a thing I found wretched, a thing I still believed was born, in part or in whole, of betrayal.

But, as it turned out, my fear was unfounded. My mind registered my line brothers the same way it registered my brothers in blood. In fact, the closer I grew to them, the less I worried about the male figures in my mind. The bond that grew between us had the same effect as being in love with a girl or feeling close to God — it pushed the unwanted figures down, but not completely out.

The same night Clay told me a truth no one else would, I was reminded of a racial truth, one conveyed to me with as much cowardice and cruelty as Clay had shown candor. The apartment where we were studying was in a mostly white section of nearby Ruston. When we were done, we all piled into cars to go back to Grambling. I got into a car with Brandon, Chopper's little brother, now one of my pledge brothers and the only other freshman.

On the way, we stopped at a convenience store. I noticed a police cruiser parked out past the gas pumps, but thought nothing of it. We weren't doing anything wrong. Everyone bought their snacks, got back into their cars, and drove away. Brandon and I were the last to leave. The cruiser pulled out as we did and started to tail us. Brandon noticed and began to drive slowly and deliberately. We said nothing. Our anxiety filled the air.

Just before we left Ruston's city limits, the cruiser's flashing lights came on. We pulled off the highway and into a subdivision. A white police officer got out of the cruiser and approached on the driver's side. Brandon took his license from his wallet and motioned to me to get the insurance and registration from the glove box. When I opened the box, a plastic switchblade comb fell out. It was like the one the Fonz had on *Happy Days,* the kind you could win if your hand was steady with the claw-crane fairway game at the parish fair.

The officer drew his gun. My hands instinctively went up as the rest of my body froze. Then, realizing that it was just a comb, a smile of relief spread across my face. I told him what it was and slowly lowered one hand to push the button to make the comb pop out. I thought it was funny. The officer did not. He was now visibly irritated. He commanded me to "drop the weapon," although I wasn't holding it, and it wasn't a weapon. He told Brandon to exit the car.

Brandon did as asked, but insisted on knowing why we had been stopped. The officer gave a reason: not signaling before a turn. It wasn't true. We hadn't made a turn before his flashing lights came on. Brandon protested, to a point. Then the officer said something I will never forget: that if he wanted to, he could make us lie down in the middle of the road and shoot us in the back of the head and no one would say anything about it. With that, he walked back to his car and drove away.

By suggesting that he could kill us right then and there, he wanted to impress upon us his power and our worth, or lack thereof. We were shocked, afraid, humiliated, and furious. We were the good guys, we thought — dean's list students with academic scholarships. I was the freshman class president. This wasn't supposed to happen to us.

As a child, I had been taught, in subtle ways, to be leery of the police. It wasn't that they were all rotten, but you didn't want to rustle around in that barrel and come upon a bad one. This was the first time I fully understood that message.

In the weeks before our line actually "came out," publicly and officially, our hazing went on "underground" — we were cut off from the world. The beatings became more frequent and more severe. Some pledges flinched and cowered, broke and cried. Others stepped up and stood tall, toeing the line for those who couldn't.

In response to the paddlings, we each developed the "pledge ass" — inch-thick, saucer-sized pads of damaged tissue and damaged nerves that formed just beneath the skin of each butt cheek, swelling so fast that they produced stretch marks. It was the way our bodies defended themselves — ensuring that we could take more blows without feeling them so intensely — or telling us that they'd had enough.

We learned to walk in line with military precision. We learned long, complicated greetings — for the Brothers as a whole and each Brother individually. And we learned to sing mournful pledge songs that recalled another time, a time of dread and drudgery, enduring and overcoming, echoing the unbreakable slaves, gandy dancers, and the black church. One of the few songs the Brothers sang to us, "I Got a Feeling," was set to the tune of "Wade in the Water," with the refrain "God's a-gonna trouble the water" replaced with "Somebody's tryin' to sneak in my frat." Every time they sang that line, I couldn't shake the feeling that it referred to me.

We bought multiple sets of matching outfits because pledges always had to be dressed alike — khakis and button-downs and bur-gundy penny loafers and matching briefcases — everything exactly the same for all of us, even our underwear.

The Brothers gave us line names that said something about the way they saw us. Mine was Picasso because I could draw and paint. I didn't know much about the actual Picasso, so I looked him up in the library. The name was more appropriate than any of us realized. Picasso once said, "Everything you can imagine is real." I was living my life by this formulation, making real the self of my imagination. The only other name I remember is the one they gave Brandon: Butter, because they thought him soft. Whenever they said "Butter!" Brandon had to chime "Parkay," like the margarine in the television commercial.

Chopper, we were told, had been particularly cruel in his hazing of previous lines, so many of the Brothers saw his little brother Brandon as a means of retribution. I didn't know what it might mean for me, Chopper being my booster and all, but I figured it did not stand me in good stead.

During that time, the Brothers found out that I didn't drink — never had — and they forced alcohol on me. Pledge Juice, they called it, cheap, mint-flavored liquor that went down hard. It took only a few swigs to loosen me, like my body was remembering something, an echo, or awakening to something, a birthright. The liquor left me lightheaded and Jell-O-kneed, like a loose-wallet man slinking out of a cathouse — feeling just right and all kinds of wrong. I now better understood how my father succumbed to it. It was a respite from worry, a rotgut way out, time deliriously spent, time unconcerned with the true costs to be paid later. I better understood the little lies that liquor told, lifting spirits and drowning sorrows while withholding the whole truth — that, in the end, it is the spirit in peril of drowning. Sorrows have gills.

The Brothers got a local woodworker to cut seventeen hand-sized pieces of wood in the shape of a scroll. Since I was Picasso, I led the painting of them — the fraternity's Greek letters going down the middle and each pledge's line number at the bottom.

After about four weeks, our debut day arrived. We gathered in a parking lot near the football practice field, all dressed alike. The Brothers tied the wooden scrolls we had painted around our necks with leather shoelaces. We were told never to take our scrolls off. We would need them, as well as our Brains, to "cross over" from pledge to full Brother, they told us. We were now official pledges.

They lined us up, put masks over our faces to extend the mystery until the very last moment, and gave us our instructions: "We better hear you muthafuckas singing on the other side of this damn campus!"

We marched, singing our pledge songs as loudly as we could, toward the girls' dorms on the other side of campus. By the time we got to the first dorm, hundreds of girls had poured into the street, excited to see who had made the line. We could barely move, hemmed in as we were by the crush of the crowd. The Brothers removed our masks, and the girls screamed and pointed and catcalled at boys they knew. I heard one person complain, "What is the freshman class president doing on line? I didn't know freshmen could pledge."

We went from dorm to dorm, singing our songs and soaking up the adulation, until the Brothers led us back to the boys' side of campus. The fun part of the evening had ended. Now it was time for the worst of it. They instructed us to meet them at a secluded, mud-holed oil field, across the interstate from a glass factory, three miles east of campus near the town of Simsboro.

We drove slowly to the field in a dreadful caravan, single file, the way cars follow a hearse with a coffin in its hollow. The other boys smoked weed and drank liquor, straight from the bottle, trying to make their bodies numb, fretting over an impending beating more extreme than we could imagine. Since I didn't smoke or drink — other than when the Brothers forced me — I had nothing.

As we turned into the field, our hearts sank. The gravel crackled under the wheels and we fell quiet. There was a horde of restless Brothers, including Brothers from other schools, milling about in front of a row of parked cars. When they saw us, they started jumping and hooting, slapping on our cars, taunting us through the windows.

This was going to be bad.

We got out, and after a few formalities, it was on. As the oil field pump jacks bobbed up and down like giant metal birds pecking the ground, we were subjected to a brutal, unfettered, gladiator-style hazing session. We were all caught in a mind-spin of madness, doing what decades of Brothers defined as the right way to make new members.

The night air was punctuated by the swats of paddles and sticks and two-by-fours, by slaps of hands on flesh, by groans of pain and by shouts of "Come on, muthafucka!" from Brothers who lost themselves in the frenzy.

This is how legends were made. The Brothers who were most inventive, brutal, or relentless were called Massive Hazers. Some Brothers revered them; others thought their behavior unseemly.

The session may have lasted half an hour, though it felt like forever. When it was over, we got back in our cars and drove away — a few bleeding, most covered in mud, everyone exhausted. I could feel the puff of my lip, the place where it had split, and I could taste the blood leaking from it, that strange metallic taste like sucking on a penny. But I smiled with a perverse pride. We all did. They told us this was as bad as it got, and we had survived. But they lied. It would get worse.

9

Hell Week

After about three weeks of marching and singing and bonding and beatings, including one more trip to the oil field, it was time for Hell Week, the last week of pledging. We were told that this would be the week without rules. And, since there were no rules, many of my line brothers took to hiding from the Brothers all day.

But I couldn't hide. I had a math class just before lunch with Joshua, our assistant dean of pledges. He made me walk with him every day from class to "the Spot," a stretch of sidewalk in front of the cafeteria onto which the Brothers had painted the fraternity's crest, and where the Brothers gathered at mealtimes to pose and preen like roosters atop a hen house. It's also where we line brothers were made to stand and sing and dance and kowtow and perform any other act of public humiliation the Brothers could imagine.

That day, as Joshua and I turned the corner by the cafeteria, my heart sank. None of my line brothers were there, only three of the Massive Hazers: Malik, his roommate Calvin, and Sean, a Brother who had pledged on the same line as Kaboom. Malik, the most notorious of them, was the kind of boy who talked the way one might expect the devil to talk: saying menacing things with a smile, his eyes always a little bloodshot, as if he had been drinking even when he hadn't, looking like he wanted to help you and hurt you at the same time.

"Come on, Blow, let's take a ride." Malik opened the door of his car. "The coupe seats twenty," he always joked, room for him, his roommate, and all my line brothers. I thought for sure that once I got into that car, I would be taken for a beating, but I couldn't refuse. I got in. So did Malik, Calvin, Sean, and Joshua. "Let's find some of your line brothers, Blow," Malik said with that sinister smile. "I know you know where they are."

It became clear to me then that they didn't really want to bother me anymore. During the pledge period I'd taken my share of punishment and hadn't flinched or cried or broken from pain. I worked hard and learned quickly. I volunteered for extra tasks and helped my line brothers finish theirs. Some Brothers even called me Super Pledge. Now they were most interested in targeting the line brothers they thought hadn't taken their fair share of punishment, those in danger of "skating into the bond," or those still prone to display weakness.

I knew that some of my line brothers were probably at one of the "safe houses" we had established while pledging, but I refused to take Malik there. I told him that I didn't know where the others were. He told me that we were going to ride around until I took him to someone. So I told him to drive me to my dorm, where, as they already knew, two of my line brothers — Marlon and Dexter — lived.

First I went to Marlon's room. He was the boy right in front of me on the line, number 12. He was a pudgy boy, fidgety and quick to sweat.

With the Brothers standing behind me, looking over my shoulder, I gave the secret knock, one my line brothers and I had devised. If you heard this knock, you were not supposed to open the door. It meant that the pledge doing the knocking was with Brothers.

But Marlon opened the door, in his underwear. The Brothers rushed him, demanding that he get dressed. I stood there dumbfounded. Why had he opened the door? I had used the secret knock. He didn't have to get caught. Then again, Marlon wasn't the sharpest boy. Truth was, he seemed the kind of guy who didn't know cat shit from candy.

Next we were off to Dexter's room, one floor down. Dexter was shorter, number 7 in line, who looked like an old man and talked like a preacher. This time I used the secret knock more obviously. But, again to my surprise, Dexter responded, "Who is it?"

"It's us, scrub. Open the door!" one of the Brothers yelled. "Scrub" was what they called all pledges, a derision that robbed the pledge of all worth. Dexter said nothing and did nothing. Now I was angry. Dexter shouldn't have answered, but now that he had, he needed to open the door. "Dexter, they know you're in there!" I yelled. Dexter didn't make a sound.

"So, he just gone leave y'all hanging," Malik said, shaking his head in disappointment, the way he always seemed to do when talking about us pledges. "See, that's the problem: y'all boys ain't been pledged right. Come on, let's go."

We walked back downstairs and got in the car, and the four Brothers drove Marlon and me to an isolated gravel road running past an expanse of standing water just off campus. There was a cardboard box in the middle of the road. Malik stopped the car. The Brothers got out and inspected the box, then called for us to get out and look. The box was filled with kittens. Marlon and I stood over the box, waiting.

Then one of the Brothers said, "Y'all have a choice. You can get your asses beat or you can throw that box of kittens in that water with that dead dog." I turned to examine the water, and indeed the carcass of a dog was rotting in it. "So what's up? What's the answer? Snap it off."

Pledges were always supposed to speak in unison — one voice, one answer. Whoever was the lowest line number among any group snapped his fingers so that all the pledges could begin speaking at the same time. Marlon was ahead of me on the line, so he had to snap for us to speak.

Snap.

"Yes," Marlon said. "No," I said at the same time.

"What?" the Brothers barked. Now they were angry. Differing answers were not allowed. "Y'all muthafuckas better figure this shit out!"

Marlon and I turned to look at each other, both of us confused and a bit upset with the other. We huddled. "What are you doing, Marlon? We can't drown those kittens," I said. "Blow, it's those fucking cats or us," Marlon huffed. Before we could settle our disagreement, the Brothers demanded a new answer, one answer.

Marlon snapped. "Yes," he said again. "No," I said again. Again we huddled. Again he snapped. Again we delivered the discordant responses.

The Brothers, frustrated, placed the box in my hands. "Blow, since you keep saying no, either throw the kittens in the water or you walk in there with that damn dog yourself," one of them said.

I looked down into the box full of helpless trembles, faint mewing, and the same sad eyes as the kitten in the picture above Uncle Paul's bed, and I turned and started walking toward the water. There was no way that I was going to drown those kittens, beating or no. And besides, I had seen so many dead things in my life that the dog didn't bother me one bit. I would wade into the water and hold the box of kittens up out of it.

As I was about to take my first step into the water, the Brothers yelled, "Stop!" Then, "This was a test. Blow, you passed. Marlon, you failed. Get in the car." I put the box down by the side of the road and went back to the car.

I now suspected that the Brothers had probably placed the box of kittens in the road before we supposedly happened upon it. I wondered whether the Brothers would circle back to get them. Or would they be able to climb out of the box? How long could they survive if no one returned for them?

As I worried about the kittens, the car pulled into a cemetery far off the highway. We all got out. The Brothers got their paddles out of the trunk. As they made me drink Pledge Juice, they savagely beat Marlon. My anger at Marlon's cowardice — his willingness to drown the kittens to save himself — quickly dissolved into empathy and unease. He didn't deserve this, no matter his mistake. I tried repeatedly to intercede, to take some of the blows for him, as we had been taught to do, but the Brothers wouldn't allow it.

Marlon took more blows that day than I'd ever seen another person take — the beating pushing far beyond making a point or toughening a pledge and into something truly maleficent. In the middle of the beating, Calvin blurted out, "I like this shit more than sex!" The other Brothers turned in disbelief and laughed at him for the sadistic implication of the remark. He insisted he was joking. I wasn't so sure. When they were done — short of breath and drenched in sweat and cruelty — Marlon could barely stand without using my shoulder for support.

A few days later, as I was getting some sleep in my dorm room — a rare occurrence during Hell Week — the phone rang. Groggy and without thinking, I answered it. That was a no-no. Answering a phone could get you in big trouble.

It was Marlon. "Blow, come get us! We at Malik's crib!"

"Aiight."

Damn, I thought. Why was he calling me? How did he get caught, again?

I threw on some clothes and drove over, expecting him and which-ever line brothers he was with to be waiting and ready to jump into the car. But when I pulled up I saw no one, just a bunch of Brothers' cars. I knew immediately that it was a group hazing session.

Impulse said to turn and leave; honor said otherwise.

I walked up to the door. I could hear the yelling, the *thwops*, the commotion, the loud music that was not able to drown it all out. My heart sank.

I knocked on the door. Everyone got quiet.

"Who is it?!"

"Blow."

Calvin opened the door with a scowl, his chest heaving, his breath short. The air inside was humid and rank from the smell of sweaty bodies and all-but-broken ones. He grabbed me and snatched me inside. As we passed through the living room I could see DJ Mardi Gras on my right, being forced to drink his own vomit from a blender because he had thrown up the original concoction he'd been given back into the container. On my left, a boy named Don was stretched out on the sofa, half conscious, convulsing like a sprayed roach, being fanned. He had taken so many "cymbals" that his ears were bleeding. Cymbals was what the Brothers called boxing your ears with the slap of open hands as hard as they could, like they were crashing cymbals.

This was crazy. It was a nest of Massive Hazers. Situations like this were so much worse than the chapter-sanctioned hazing sessions at the oil field, where the Massive Hazers were somewhat constrained by more moderate Brothers. At the oil field, the chapter officers' unofficial job was to make sure that no one got severely injured, so the home chapter wouldn't get in serious trouble. But no officers were present on nights like this.

When I got to the back of the room I saw Nash. Oh no, I thought.

"Come on, scrub. Bend that ass ova," Nash said, directing me into the cut for a paddling.

Oh no, I thought again. My wallet was in my back pocket. That was a mistake pledges were taught never to make. The Brothers took wallets. I tried to sneak it out and into my front pocket, but Nash noticed. "Wait a minute. Give me that. Hell, yeah," he said.

His eyes darted around the room, and he grabbed me, Dexter, and Marlon and ushered us outside and into my car. Nash flipped through my wallet, pocketed the lone twenty, and then took out my bank card. "Let's go to the bank, Blow." I searched for a lie to protect my bank account, which had quite a bit of money in it, from unspent scholarship funds and work-study pay.

"Big Brother, that card is on my mother's account, and she's watching it. She knows I'm on line. If I take money out, she's going to know something is up."

Nash frowned and stared at me from under his bushy brows, knowing that I was probably lying but unwilling to risk creating a problem with the college or the national fraternity this late in the pledge period.

"Aiight then, let's go. You gone buy me some beer and somethin' to eat."

We went to the largest grocery store in town and did some shopping. I paid. We got our bags, got back in the car, and drove to Nash's house, a small, rundown trailer in the back row of a poorly maintained trailer park. When we pulled up to the trailer Nash said, "Where's Brandon? I want him!"

All the Brothers wanted Brandon — apart from the payback for his older brother's cruel treatment of previous pledges, Brandon was full of excuses and always found ways to be safely away from the group.

"We don't know, Big Brother."

We took the groceries inside, then Nash said, "Aiight, Blow and Dexter, you go find Brandon. Marlon, you stay here. You ain't goin' nowhere till I get Brandon."

By now the sky was turning the pastel colors of morning, heralding the rising sun. Dexter and I had no idea where Brandon was. But this time I was earnestly searching. I wanted to find Brandon and force him into the car. I figured that boys like Marlon had taken more than enough beatings, and Brandon had avoided many. If I had to deliver Brandon to save Marlon that morning, I intended to do it.

Dexter and I went to the trailer park where Brandon's girlfriend lived. I got out and knocked on the door. She said Brandon wasn't there. I figured she was probably lying, but there was nothing I could do about it.

But when I turned to walk back to the car, I saw that Dexter had opened the door, fallen out onto the ground, and started a slow army crawl, on his stomach, knees, and elbows.

I walked beside him, yelling at him to get up.

"Dexter! What you doin'?! Get up! We gotta go!"

"I can't do this shit no mo', Blow."

"What?! Dexter, get the fuck up off that ground!"

"I can't do this shit no mo'!"

"Fuck it!" I said.

I went back to my car, got in, slammed the door, and peeled out. I looked back through my rearview mirror, watching Dexter crawl in the middle of the street as darkness gave way to light. I was going to have to do this alone.

But my frantic search to find Brandon and save Marlon was failing, and my failure gave way to exhaustion and anger just as I was passing Kaboom's house. I decided that if I couldn't save Marlon, Kaboom, as our dean of pledges, needed to. He came to the door at my urgent knocking, not happy to see me. I spilled out what happened at the crazy hazing session, about Mardi Gras and the vomit, Don and the cymbals, Dexter crawling in the road, and the fact that Marlon was still being held at Nash's house. "Somebody is gonna get hurt."

"This is Hell Week. I'm not the DP this week. Ain't no rules." And with that Kaboom closed the door.

Okay, if there were no rules, then it was on. I drove back to Nash's house. I was going to rescue Marlon . . . somehow. I knocked on the door. A girl's voice purred, "Come in." Nash's girlfriend was lying on the couch watching Marlon dance, which he was doing with only one shoe on, Nash's idea of entertainment. He had taken Marlon's other shoe to make sure he didn't run away.

"Where's Nash?" I asked.

"He's asleep," Marlon said, still dancing.

"Asleep? Then let's get the fuck outta here!" I said.

"But what about my shoe?" Marlon asked.

"Fuck your shoe!"

The girl seemed nonplused and said nothing.

As we turned to leave, I saw the collection of Brains and scrolls that Nash had stolen, arranged like hunting trophies on a brass-and-glass shelf by the door.

Each pledge needed his Brain and his scroll to cross over, but giving these items such importance made them targets of all manner of foul play and skullduggery on the part of the Brothers, who tried to get them from us so that they could demand a ransom for their return.

My own scroll had been stolen by a Brother named Adam, who lived in the honors dorm. He knew that I was on scholarship and needed to keep up my grades, so he told me I could come by his room to study during the day if I needed to. I felt a regional kinship with him — he was from Shreveport, about forty miles from Gibsland — and took him up on his offer.

One day in his room he asked me how I was holding up. I let down my guard and began talking to him. Then, without warning, swoosh! In an instant he had grabbed my scroll and swung a razor blade to cut the taut leather strap that held it around my neck.

"That's right, muthafucka! Got yo' shit! You gone have to pay me to get this shit back!"

I stood there stunned. Never mind the scroll — he had just swung a razor blade a couple of inches from my jugular. What if I had flinched?

I had to pay Adam $60 to get the scroll back, and I never looked at him the same way again.

I saw now that Nash had more of our Brains and scrolls than I could count. He stood to collect hundreds of dollars in ransom. Why should my line brothers have to pay, I thought. I grabbed them all. "No rules." Marlon and I broke for the door, got in the car, and peeled out. I knew that Nash wouldn't stop until he'd made me pay for my thievery, but I didn't care.

This might have seemed a small thing to some, this bucking of rules in the midst of a brutal survival game, but to me it was a revelation. It was the first time I had taken a bold action, though it would surely bring me harm. It was the first time I realized that my strength was rooted not only in long-suffering but also in risk-taking. I came closer to crossing over into manhood that morning at Nash's.

Luckily for me, Nash was arrested for an outstanding warrant shortly thereafter. When we heard the news, my line brothers and I jumped and shouted, especially me.

A couple of weeks later, at the fraternity house, we officially entered the brotherhood. It was a rather anticlimactic ceremony, but after came the emotion. Boys who had been on opposite ends of beatings embraced on the same side of membership — laughing and crying, chanting and drinking. It was a time of rejoicing and release, to celebrate completion and new beginnings. All was supposed to be forgiven, the hazing not to be seen as personal but as an essential part of the process. No gripes. No grudges.

On this I failed. I would absolve the moderates but always look askance at the Massive Hazers, especially Nash.

10

The Champagne-Colored Girl

The summer after pledging was my summer of listlessness, a time spent mostly resting—trying to let my body recover from weeks of sleepless nights and stressful days.

One of the few things I remember was a ride home from Houston with my mother. Nathan had moved there after college to work with Grandpa Bill on the railroad. That summer Nathan had been badly burned while working on a car when the radiator erupted, and we had gone to visit so that my mother could help nurse him back to health.

On our way back home to Gibsland, somewhere among the one-horse towns and hundred-head cattle ranches of east Texas, my mother spoke.

She told me she had seen a real difference in me, that I was growing up, that I was becoming a man. Among the things left unsaid was that she was proud of me. Proud. Of me. But she didn't have to say the words for me to hear them. And she didn't hide the emotion of it in a joke, the way we often did. It stood, naked and tender and true.

I didn't know whether to puff up with pride or collapse in tears.

I had done the one thing that I wanted most to do since the day that I ran across the basketball court and she laid into me: I had removed that fright from her eyes and silenced the worry in her rebuke. I had pushed down that part of me that so offended folks. My mother could now breathe freely, even if it meant that I was left gasping for air.

In the fall, I returned to school thinking that I could acclimate to my new perch as a Brother. I moved off campus again, renting an apartment with a Brother who had just transferred to Grambling from another school. At our first chapter meeting, we held elections. Instead of starting with the lower offices, we started with the most important — president. I sat on the floor in a corner as two other Brothers were nominated, trying to decide which would get my vote. I settled on the guy everyone called Cake, a round-faced boy who walked knock-kneed, like it was intentional and cool. He was older and respected among the Brothers, and he was Chopper's roommate.

Then something happened I hadn't foreseen: Kaboom nominated me. I was flattered but taken aback. What did I know about the workings of the fraternity? I wasn't only a new member, I was also the youngest member. Besides, I had been reelected class president while I was on line, a sympathy vote no doubt, and that would keep me plenty busy.

We nominees had to step out of the room for the discussion and vote. Cake was so sure he was going to win that he told me and the other nominee that he definitely wanted us to work with him to move the bond forward. I was sure he was going to win too, so I nodded my agreement. Soon the door opened and the Brothers waved us back in.

Someone said, "Congratulations, Bro. Blow, our neophyte president."

What? Surely there was some mistake. But there was no mistake. I had won, mostly on the strength of my line brothers' votes. Kaboom had often told us when we were on line that, because there were seventeen of us, if we voted as a block we could have our way, and that is exactly what happened.

The tradition was that the exiting president would visit the entering one, turn over all fraternity business, and give advice. So the exiting president, a tall, hulky boy with small wire-rimmed glasses called Big Hoss, who was from a small town just north of Gibsland and always called me homeboy, visited me the next week at my apartment.

When we were pledges, the Brothers had stressed to us that "the bond is a business," so I expected the chapter's records to be in order. But they weren't. For instance, Big Hoss couldn't tell how much money we'd raised the year before or how it had been spent.

I decided that if the ideal was for the bond to be run like a business, I would run it at peak efficiency. I got the back statements from the bank and audited the chapter's finances. I realized that we made most of our money from paid parties after football games — as much at $3,000 a party — but that there was no consistency as to which games would be followed by a party. I decided they all should be — no need to leave money on the table.

At the parties, I worked the door to ensure that our dress code, "dress to impress," was enforced — no jeans, no sneakers. To make sure no trouble erupted, we hired off-duty police officers, and we never served alcohol. Our logic was that girls wanted a safe place to go where they could dress up and dance with equally well-dressed guys without fear or fights. The strategy worked. Our parties were always packed with pretty girls, so much so that they often complained that there weren't enough boys to dance with. That was one of the perks of being one of the Pretty Boys, another reason to endure the beatings: the never-ending stream of girls, mostly those enamored of the idea of us.

The girls and their attention caught me off guard.

My nights were rarely lonely, my bed rarely empty. I was being chosen, constantly. There were so many I could hardly keep track. Only a few stood out: the ones I truly fell for and the quirky ones. There was the half-white daughter of the Chicago militant who smiled like the Cheshire cat. The ex–ballet dancer with the quick-to-bleed toes. The Compton-born foster child. The girl with the pacemaker. The bookish girl with the glasses who showed up on my doorstep wearing a trench coat and nothing else. The half-Asian girl on a mission to "sow her wild oats" before marriage who kept a list of prospective conquests, a list I was on.

All the girls and the strong friendships I developed with my fraternity brothers overtook the male apparitions. The relief of that absence, and the sheer volume of girls, allowed me for the first time to discern what I truly liked in a lover: lightness. Lightness of body and lightness of spirit, girls who played with a gossamer-fine femininity, twirling it around the ends of their fingers like a cloud of cotton candy, the kind that melted with the touch of a tongue. I had been around heavy women all my life – all weight and worry and anger – women who warned of pistols in purses, girls who boasted of being quick to "cut a fool" and "snatch a bitch." I craved the opposite.

There was one girl who stood out above all others. Her name was Greta. We met during my listless summer, when I was recuperating from pledging. Chopper, another of our fraternity brothers, and I had gone to a nightclub in Shreveport. Once inside, Chopper and the other boy quickly found girls and headed to the dance floor. I stood around the edges; nightclubs made me ill at ease.

I wasn't a conventionally handsome boy like most of the other Brothers. Puberty had pulled and stretched me since the Ringgold pageant judges crowned me the black Little Master. I was tall and wiry. My nose was long and spread wide at the nostrils. My head was large and my face gaunt, like President Lincoln's profile on a penny. The attributes I was most confident about – smarts, resourcefulness, resilience, proper etiquette – didn't register in a noisy nightclub.

That night I asked a few girls if they wanted to dance, and each demurred in that way that said, "Yes, but not with you." I didn't know how to speak in the dulcet tones that wound-up men speak to holdout women, so I stood watching everyone else dance, until I spotted one of the most striking girls I had ever seen.

She was part Creole, the color of champagne, with light brown eyes that sparkled even in the darkness. But for some reason my eyes set on her hair. It was stiffer than that of other girls who looked like her. It was the kind of hair that works against a brush, the kind that stubbornly holds a shape when it's ironed, the kind that could only grow a hand's length before it broke off, no matter how much care you took.

She was dancing alone and smiling—a broad smile, showing too much of the gums. I built up my courage, approached her, and asked her to dance. "Yes," she said, to my surprise. She was from Shreveport, just graduated from high school, and had sneaked into the club with her older sister to celebrate. I told her where I was from and why I was there, whatever I could get out between the dances and over the music. She seemed as taken with me as I was with her, which I found hard to believe. Soon her sister came for her, but the girl didn't want to go. She wanted to stay with me. With me! But the sister insisted, so the girl wrote her name and telephone number on a napkin and headed toward the door, disappearing into the crowd the way a special marble blends into a bag of many. I looked down at the paper: "Greta," along with seven digits scrawled in careless block lettering—the sloppy kind of writing that would get your knuckles rapped in grade school.

In the weeks that followed, I called a few times and tried to arrange a date, but she always seemed to be busy. I assumed that the heat from that night had cooled, that what I had felt from her was a random flirtation, not actual interest.

But that September I saw Greta again. She was a Grambling freshman and was at one of the back-to-school block parties, hanging with a group of other pretty girls. One of them was a high-strung, preternatural beauty named Erica Wright, whom the world would soon come to know as the singer Erykah Badu, "the queen of neo-soul." I found out that Greta was running for Miss Freshman, and, having run for a freshman office myself, I figured I had a great way to strike up a conversation and jog her memory about our night in the club.

I approached, said "Hi," and asked if she remembered me. Greta giggled and said "No," though I was sure she did, only I was even less impressive in the sobriety of sunlight. Before I could gather myself, she disappeared. I was hurt and angry and vowed to myself that I would never allow her to forget the snub.

She won the election and became part of Miss Grambling's court, which meant that we'd spend a lot of time traveling together that year. But I did my best to pretend I was unimpressed by her, and uninterested. No one knows how to hold a grudge like a proper Southerner. She began to make advances, but I assumed she was only making fun of my contrived antipathy. Besides, she already had a boyfriend. But as the year wore on, her overtures became more urgent, until finally it occurred to me that she was sincere.

Soon our clandestine meetings began. I had fallen in love with her the night I met her, even if I had tried to forget it and deny it. That night she had come into me like a cloud of milk first introduced to coffee — stirring beneath the surface of me, bringing lightness and taking away the bitterness. The idea that she might love me back was almost overwhelming. After the trials of pledging, I had come to believe that the toughest part of me was the best part of me, the way folks say sugarcane is sweetest at the joint, but Greta seemed to value something I thought I had left back in Gibsland.

I remember the first time we kissed, not because there were many sparks, but because there were few. Greta moved my spirit more than my flesh, the opposite of what some of the other girls had done. I loved Greta in a different way, a deeper way, the way bodies come together more for completion than passion. There was something searching and tender in the way I touched her, the way you touch a body to be sure you are awake and not dreaming. I was at home when I was with her. My spirit loved this girl in a way that it had never loved another. It was a deep-in-the-bones love, the kind where you ache when you are apart. With her I relaxed, exhaled, forgot myself, and became myself. We laughed all the time, at everything and nothing, a giddy, punch-drunk response to the realization that we had found another who could truly see us, know us, read us.

We let down our guard and lay naked and vulnerable in each oth-er's arms — as naked and vulnerable as I could allow at that phase of my life. The more we talked, the more I understood that her wounds were as deep as mine, only different, which drew me to her even more — me marveling at our matching scars. As with most girls who chose me, she saw in me an echo of her father — smart and distant — a boy tasked with renewing her faith in men. We were both searching for redemption and validation, aiming higher than our station, pretending to be more refined than our families and histories supported. In fact, I lost sight of where I ended and she began, the way you can lose the line where clear skies meet calm seas.

We spoon-fed each other's narcissism, fanned the flames of each other's ambition, counseled each other on problems, shielded each other's weaknesses, held each other's secrets — many of them, though not all.

She was not willing to be mine, not completely. She overtly held a bit of herself back, as I secretly did the same. She was somebody else's girlfriend and always would be during the years that we crept around in the shadows, through the late-night pickups and predawn drop-offs. I pretended that was the way I wanted it, because that was the way she insisted it be. But that, for me, was a lie. I wanted her more than she wanted me, and that fact increasingly injured my pride.

The time that she gave to me, she stole from him. I often wondered what she whispered in his ear after spending the night in my bed. It was hard for me to reconcile, that she loved me enough to risk her rela-tionship with him, but not enough to forswear it. This kept up until one day she came to my apartment to tell me that she had made up her mind to be faithful to the boy who believed she loved only him. I pretended that I agreed, and that it was all for the best, but when she left, my heart broke.

I became convinced that love would be unattainable for a boy like me, that it would pass me over in this life, and that I needed to make my peace with that.

Soon, the weight of being the fraternity's president — the thing I believed had taken me as far away from the boy I had been as it was possible for me to be — became more of a burden than a badge. During my two years in the post we had two ugly brawls with other Grambling fraternities. The first brawl, which landed our chapter on probation, started at a party another fraternity — the nerdy boys — was having. There was some confusion at the door about whether one of my fraternity brothers had paid his admission. It ended horribly in the parking lot, with the police indiscriminately spraying Mace and with several combatants suffering injuries so serious they had to be taken to the hospital. The second brawl, which earned us a suspension, started with a flagrant foul during an intramural basketball game. The other fraternity — the country boys — was playing rough, taunting us "pretty boys." By the last foul we had had enough. The benches cleared and the fighting spilled out into the street, with people threatening to pull guns.

At the same time, a sophomore from the Bronx with a congenital heart defect died at Morehouse College in Atlanta during an "underground" hazing session. A few months later, the National Pan-Hellenic Council, the governing body of all historically black Greek-letter organizations, met and decided to ban pledging altogether. There would now be a two-week "membership intake process" instead.

Young Brothers were furious. They saw the elders who made the decision as hypocrites and apostates — virtually all of them had been hazed and had been hazers themselves when they were younger. And young Brothers saw the decision as a desperate business move by those who feared — rightly — that hazing lawsuits posed an existential monetary threat to the organization. There was nothing young Brothers despised more than the idea that the fraternity was choosing corporate interests over cultural ones.

From the moment we crossed over, older Brothers had groomed us — to change us from victims of hazing to perpetuators of it. They often shared hazing stories over drinks, explaining to us how important the practice was to proper pledging, how transformational moments had to be forced, how it was each Brother's duty to continue the practice. Brothers had to make pledging physically difficult so that the bond would be stronger — the bond between individual pledges and the bond between them and us. Unspoken in it all, the subtext, was that the hazing, with its brutality and physical hardships, was supposed to connect us to ancestral suffering, providing a generational throughline of punishment and perseverance, from bondage to fraternal bonding. Thus, the Brothers saw no wrong in it, only honor and heritage, and we were easily indoctrinated into that warped way of thinking. The only dishonorable hazers were the Massive Hazers, whom everyone had an obligation to constrain.

Since the no-pledging decision came down while I was president, I had to help find a way to balance Brothers' desire to "follow tradition" with our directive to follow the new rules. It could not be done. In the end, the other officers and I, blinded by the brotherhood, voted to perform the entire pledge process "underground," so that we could retain much of the hazing and our local rituals. The pledging ban only served to make the entire process more unsupervised, uneven from chapter to chapter, and dangerous. Now many of our fraternity's chapters increasingly focused on massive midnight hazing sessions, like the ones our chapter carried out at the oil field.

Inviting other chapters to hazing sessions was a way of building bonds among schools — pledges rarely forgot a visiting chapter — and of assuring other chapters that traditions were being upheld at the home chapter, that "your boys" were being "made right." It was also how outlawed hazing practices spread — chapter to chapter, in the dark of night, like a virus.

I wasn't a major hazer — it was not my temperament, and as president, it was not my job — but neither was I a minor one. I never hit boys with paddles or sticks or two-by-fours, but I did haze with my hands when pledges didn't try hard enough or failed at a task. I took no joy in it. I was simply lowering myself to what was expected of me, what we had been convinced was required. And by hazing only in the promotion of training, I crafted for myself a digestible rationale.

The truth was that the hazing worked as advertised — it broke a boy to the point that he was forced to lean on his line brothers to survive it. It was a group trauma, and it bound people together the way trauma often does. Hazing reduced pledges to their weakest and most vulnerable and demanded that they rise from it, forcing them to summon strength greater than they knew they possessed, the way it had done for me. The process would produce some of the most durable and loyal friendships of my life.

The problem was that for those being hazed it was also terribly hazardous, and occasionally deadly. And for those doing the hazing it was just as troubling: it was morally corrosive. The intentions sometimes may have been honorable, but the actions were not. Hazing unleashed the beast in a boy, granted unbridled permission to do the unthinkable, shielding heinous behavior behind a screen of righteousness. The truth is that no one is held harmless in the commission of cruelty. With every blow, I surrendered a bit of myself.

At a hazing session at the University of Louisiana in Monroe, nearly forty miles east of Grambling, the local Brothers assembled us in a wide-open field off a seldom-traveled road. The dean of pledges gathered his charges — a knot of bowed heads and stiffened bodies standing as close together as possible, for whatever protection or solace that might provide. I was standing with the president of that chapter, planning to help him keep a watchful eye so that no pledge was injured. After a few formalities, someone gave the signal for the session to commence. As it did, one of the pledges broke and ran. Coward!, I thought, and ran after him. I hadn't planned on hazing before the boy bolted, but I was sure now that his fleeing must not be tolerated. Our fraternity could not abide the chicken-hearted.

But the boy was faster than I was. I couldn't catch him. As I saw him pull away, something struck me. The way the boy ran reminded me of the way my father had run to flee my mother's gunshots: not flat-out running but a casual quickness, like he was smiling through his fear. Something about it chilled my anger and slowed my stride. Just as it did, I heard a jet overhead, the deep roaring whistle of the engines like a breath blown across the mouth of a Coke bottle. The plane was flying so low I was sure a sharp-eyed passenger could see us. I stood stock-still as it landed a few football fields away.

I realized that we were in a field on the approach path of the city's airport. Seeing the plane and imagining its passengers and the folks milling about in the terminals — just those images of humanity — stopped me for long enough to ask myself, What am I *doing?* I was not pleased by what had become of me. This was not the me I knew. I slowly walked back to my car, got in, and waited for the hazing session to be over.

This wasn't right. This wasn't me. I was better than this. Was this what it took to be one of the real boys, a man, to remain silent and give participatory approval to something that I knew in the pit of me was wrong? Was this the cost of other folks' respect: the loss of self-respect?

I had gone from the bottom of the male hierarchy to the top of it, and all it had required was the complete suffocation of my soul. I was at the apex of the crushing mound of social subjugation that had caused me to squeeze my seven-year-old hand into my pocket in search of a bottle of pills and a way out. I had traded a public shame for a private one — hypocrisy in place of ostracism. And somehow, in the twist of my mind, that was better. Wrestling with myself was easier than fighting the whole world. Easier. That was the word. Cowardice is always easier than bravery. Always. Bending over is always easier than standing up. Playing a man is always easier than being one.

After a few more fraternity episodes, each one seemingly more unconscionable than the last, I called a meeting near the end of my junior year and resigned my post as president. Enough.

It would take many years for me to come fully to terms with the whole of what I engaged in in the name of brotherhood. Everything about my life had made me pliable. I was fully engaged by the idea of fraternity after I became immersed in it: the focus on achievement, the idea of Brothers of my own choosing, sworn to stand with me and stand up for me, the comfort of boys and men who I was confident wanted only to befriend me and never betray me. My longings had numbed me to my wrongs. It would only be in the cold gaze of hindsight that I would be able to comprehend that while in flight from pain, I became an agent of it.

11

Lie Detector

I don't remember exactly how the CIA came to recruit me — or precisely when — but they did, around the time that I resigned as fraternity president. I was being chosen, again.

What I do recall is that the CIA came to our school each year to recruit, and once an agent came to speak to a history class I was taking. When he was done, he was peppered with silly questions, like the one from the boy who asked, "Did you guys kill JFK?" The agent responded with his own brand of deadpan humor: "I can't tell you, because if I did, I'd have to kill you."

I remember thinking that an internship with the CIA would look good on the résumé of someone who still wanted to become a lawyer before becoming a politician. They wanted me — they seemed to delight in the notion of a smart boy from the middle of nowhere — and I wanted them.

I was soon being summoned to CIA headquarters in Reston, Virginia, for a final round of interviews and tests. My only fear was that

Uncle Henry's time at Leavenworth would show up on one of the background checks and disqualify me.

The plane I took to Washington was only the second one I had been on, after my first to the international science fair.

That weekend at the CIA was a blur of serious faces and conservative suits. We prospective interns sat through meetings in which square-jawed men gave soporific speeches about what the agency stood for and what our likely jobs would be — analyzing a country or region and writing a report on it. We were interviewed and given basic physicals. Our sight and hearing were checked, mine for the first time. I was sailing through it all, sure that the internship was a lock. Until it was time to take the lie detector test.

I sat in the chair and the agent asked me a round of questions to calibrate the machine, simple questions, like what was my name. Then he began with the real ones. They were things like, "Have you ever cheated on an exam?" All seemed to be going well until two questions came, the second more stressful than the first. The first was, "Have you ever used drugs?" I answered "No," which was true, but I could hear the needle of the machine scratching "lie" on the paper and could hear the man's papers rustle as he wrote. How could this be?, I thought. Was it the guilt of sharing the weed-filled locker with Russell and Alphonso in high school? Was it my belief that I'd likely gotten a contact high from the weed my fraternity brothers smoked? What had caused the anxiety at the asking of that question?

And before I could truly recover, the second question came: "Have you ever had sex with a man?"

I hadn't thought consciously about Chester's betrayal since I joined the fraternity and began to entertain the never-ending stream of girls, but there it was now, most present. How to answer the question? Both Chester and I had been boys, not yet men at the time. It wasn't consensual. There was no penetration, so was it technically sex? The anxiety rose in me like dust from a thing long neglected and abruptly disturbed.

I could hear the needle of the machine begin to move even before I opened my mouth. I had a hundred questions, but I had to give one answer. "No," I said. The needle scratched wildly on the paper — lie.

As soon as the test was over, I turned to the man and the things that I had never let spill from my lips came pouring out. All of it. Chester and his betrayal and my guilt. But I said the words the way one speaks to a mirror, not to him, but to myself. There was no emotion in it, no release, only a search for words. When I was finished, the secret still felt kept, still balled up in my gut.

The man looked at me the way Roseanne had the day we tried to have sex and I didn't know what to do — with a mix of disappointment and disbelief. I begged him to test me again. He reluctantly allowed it.

This time I answered yes to the sex-with-a-man question, but the machine still scratched "lie" onto the paper. I thought in that moment, I will never be free. It took a machine designed to catch liars to help me see that I didn't yet know my own truth.

In that moment my dream of becoming a politician vanished. How could I be a governor if the government thought I was a liar? How was it that I had no yes-or-no answer for what had happened to me? Chester's betrayal not only had destroyed my past, but was destroying my future. I went back home and told no one what had happened, only that I would not be getting the internship. And the male figures that had largely been absent since I joined the fraternity were now back, like a pack of dogs sniffing around a kitchen door.

Soon after I returned from Virginia, our fraternity had a party. I was despondent. I didn't feel like going, but Nathan was visiting from Houston and he wanted me to take him. So I went. But I couldn't be bothered to dress up. I wore a T-shirt, shorts, and sandals, a wanton violation of our fraternity's dress code, one I'd upheld to deny hundreds of people entry to our other parties. The Brothers were befuddled and disapproving, but no one complained. Protocol dictated that an ex-president was owed the utmost deference. No one would deny me entry or chasten me. The only person who said something was Clay. He simply asked, almost under his breath, while scanning me head to toe, "So you never gonna wear hard-bottom shoes again?" He didn't need to say more. I knew that I had to snap out of it.

With only a few weeks left of school, and only one year remaining of my college life, I began to panic. I knew now that I wasn't going to law school or to pursue a career in politics. So the mass communications major I had never taken seriously, the visual communications concentration I had decided on as the easiest way to keep my scholarship and my commitment to the fraternity, would be my way to a career. But I had never tried to get work in a real newsroom. The summer of my sophomore year I had helped my brother reroof houses under the blaze of a Louisiana sun. And although I had found some things about the work fulfilling — the physical release of repetitive toil, the way it clarifies thinking — I didn't care to repeat it. So I typed up a résumé, gathered the few clips I had from the student newspaper, and sent them to the *Shreveport Times,* requesting an internship in the graphics department. At first they told me they didn't have an internship for me, but I called every day and created new charts and graphs like the ones I saw printed in their newspaper, which I sent in to impress them. Eventually they relented and granted my request.

I dove into the work that summer. I figured other people might have more training than I did, but no one had more hours in the day. I always got to the newsroom early and stayed late. And I always tried to edit and improve the little bits of copy that the news desk sent over to be included in the maps and charts and diagrams that we created on our first-generation Macintosh computers. I took on as many projects as I could, anything the permanent employees didn't want, and tried to make them sing.

The graphics boss, a soft-spoken man named Frank, encouraged me and appreciated me. He started sending me to the news meetings on behalf of the department. I loved this. Deep down, I considered myself more reporter than artist.

One day I had the epiphany that I could combine the two. I'd shown up one morning for a news meeting to find the newsroom abuzz about the death of an entire family in their home: carbon monoxide poisoning.

Frank wasn't in yet, so I couldn't ask him what to do. I followed my gut instinct and went to the scene. When I arrived, there was a stillness in the air. I immediately recognized it as the familiar quiet that hangs over a house after someone dies in it. The house was roped off and the police were milling about. I talked to one of the officers to find out what had happened: the electricity to the house had been cut off, so the father put a generator in the crawl space under the house to power the air conditioners while the family slept that hot summer night. The exhaust fumes seeped up through the floorboards and killed them all. The bodies, except for those of the small children, were found not in the beds but on the bedroom floors and in the hallway. The family members, weakened by the gas, had probably collapsed there in their attempt to escape.

I knew this story would be best told with a diagram of the house and the generator in the crawl space and where the bodies were found. But the officers wouldn't let me enter to get the layout. I did my best to peer through the windows to figure it out, but that wasn't good enough. Then I noticed that all the houses on the street looked alike. Presumably the layout of one was the layout of all.

I knocked at the house next door and asked the owner if she had ever been in the house where the people had died and if the layout was the same as her house: yes and yes. So I asked if she would give me a tour of her house so that I could sketch the floor plan, and she agreed. I then took the diagram to one of the officers and had him indicate where each of the bodies had been found. I got the name and model of the generator and went around to every sporting goods and hardware store until I found someone who sold the same model. I made a diagram of it, and had the salesman talk me through how it worked.

I rushed back to the newsroom, built my diagram on the computer, and added my captions. The paper used it on the front page. I knew then that I could be what was coming to be known as a visual journalist. It wasn't as high an ambition as being governor, but I was good at it, and I liked it.

At work things were going great, but at home Paul was going crazy.

My mother's night classes had earned her a master's degree and several certifications. And she sometimes taught GED classes after school and on weekends. This all raised her meager income to the point that she was able to build a new house in the field where Papa Joe had raised the hogs.

As it turned out, Papa Joe's house had not been Papa Joe's at all, but Big Mama's. The original house had burned down, and Big Mama had rebuilt it with the insurance money she got when her second husband died. At any rate, my mother needed something to call her own to fully come into her own.

The new house was brick, with aluminum-framed windows that held in the heat and kept out the drafts. It had two bathrooms — two! — and both had pipes built into the wall, and there were no gaps between the floor and the walls where you could see out and the world could come in. And there were locks on the doors.

When Paul went crazy, my mother took to sleeping with her door locked: "I don't want Paul to come in here on me." Crazy men were dangerous men. We knew this well. They were men like cousin Jack, who would come to my high school basketball games. Jack was a cousin by marriage, not by blood. One of my father's brothers had married his mother after his real daddy was killed one night trying to cross the interstate on foot to get to a juke joint.

Jack was a short, high-strung, wild-haired man who talked faster than you could listen, like a scratched LP record played at the speed of a 45, always repeating things. "That my cousin, that my cousin, anybody mess wit' 'im, anybody mess wit' 'im, I'll cut ya, I'll cut ya," he'd say, drawing his finger across his throat, tracing his own chin-strap scar where someone had slit his throat, but he had lived. Then Jack would laugh, not a deep laugh but the kind that forms just behind the teeth, more a nervous impulse to fill a space between thoughts than a natural reflex to something funny. "Hehehehehe."

Others laughed too, cautiously, to keep from being frozen by fear. Jack was possessed of a mercurial nature, his mood was known to suddenly shift from silly to deadly serious. His mental state was severe enough that he was on disability — getting a "crazy check," folks called it. I knew that Jack walked with a blade. I knew that he meant what he said: that if anyone bothered me, he'd gut him like a fish. This knowledge made me feel both safe and nervous around him, but luckily Jack never cut anyone for me.

Then there was the quiet boy with the kind eyes who lived across the interstate and who had graduated from high school around the same time as my brother Nathan. He slowly slipped into insanity and one day killed both his parents. When the authorities arrived, folks said, the boy was sitting on the front steps of his house like nothing had happened. When they asked him why he had done such a thing, he responded with no empathy or irony: "Why don't you go in dere and ask 'em?" My mother didn't want Uncle Paul to send anyone in to ask her dead body any questions.

We stared at Uncle Paul. He stared at nothing, with the blank, wide-eyed look of the wounded deer that we had tried to keep in the House of the Drowned Children — desperate, anxious, and confused, wanting to run away but not able to.

He waded out into the weeds behind the house, the ones he had compulsively cut and burned before, the ones he no longer cut now that the rheumatism had stiffened his joints, so much so that he had to walk with a stick. He'd make his way to the same spot every day, where he would stand motionless, like a pointing dog on the scent of game, looking up at something in the sky, something that we couldn't see.

His mind was looping back on itself, conjuring images his eyes had not seen, listening to voices his ears had not heard. He was still Paul, but not Paul. There was now a stranger in the house, out of his mind.

Paul's insanity made my depression seem inconsequential, so I tried to keep myself busy and my mind off it.

On the weekends I started hanging out at the Starlite Lounge, a particle-board juke joint at the Gibsland exit just off the interstate. This was a dangerous place. I once saw a man get chased out and into the woods across the street, where he was beaten and some say stabbed. But you could dance there and get a cheap drink and a cheap date.

One night I saw Roseanne's brother, Arthur, at the Starlite. In high school we played on the basketball team and rode motorcycles together. My bike was a Honda 150. My father had bought it, used, when I turned fifteen. It was the only thing he ever bought for me, the first time he didn't say "You jus' blew it" and did in fact follow through on his promise. I had heard that Arthur had a bad motorcycle accident. He was wearing a coat that hot August Louisiana evening inside the Starlite. I thought that odd, so I nodded at the coat and asked, "What's up?," wondering about his health and wanting an explanation. "I'm using the bathroom," he responded. Then he pulled back the coat to reveal his urostomy bag filling with piss. I never rode my motorcycle again.

Another night at the Starlite I ran into a girl who had been a cheerleader at a neighboring school when I had been the captain of our basketball team. She had the kind of face that said the "Indian" wasn't far back in her family — flat, with high, pushed-back cheekbones, leading with the chin. And her skin wasn't like other black folks' skin. It was stretched tight like there was nothing between it and the bone.

She smiled and flirted and told me that she had always liked me but had never had the nerve to tell me so. We talked and danced that night and arranged to go to the movies.

It was the beginning of a summer of midnight romps, just the diversion I needed from my depression.

One night when I picked her up for a date, she instructed me to drive out of town along a seldom-traveled road. On the way we made idle chatter and listened to music. Within minutes, the amber glow from the windows of sporadically spaced houses had completely vanished from the horizon. This stretch of the road was uninhabited for miles, except for the cows sleeping in the fields and the bugs that smashed into the car's grille. I drove slowly, reaching my hand over between her legs, massaging the inside of her thigh. We came to the top of a hill between two vast pastures.

"Stop here," she said.

I stopped in the middle of the one-lane road. She got out, took off her top, and turned to me, summoning me. She wanted to make love in the open air. I was game.

The moon was big and full and low in the cloudless sky, bathing the hilltop in functional light, like that of a cracked door on a dark room — enough to make out shapes but not colors.

We tore off all our clothes and began having loud sex all over the hood, which was nearly hot enough to burn the skin. We slipped and slid our way up the windshield, excited by the feel of the night air on our moist naked bodies and by the possibility of being caught.

When we were done, I collapsed between her thighs in a post-orgasmic paralysis, ass bare and face flushed, with nothing but the sky draped over my shoulders. I was motionless save my heaving chest, pressed into her breasts. Her delicate hands were moving slowly over my back, her fingernails tracing figure eights as she whispered sweet nothings in my ear.

I could see in that moment how wrong this was. It was the tenderness in her touch that told me that our romps meant more to her than they would ever mean to me. She was falling in love. I was just falling.

I feared that I was moving into a moral desert where the balm of attention and the thrill of passion were becoming temporary highs for a boy bereft of real connection. Mine was a heart succumbing to coldness in search of a body to remind it of warmth. I understood that I was being selfish, so I stopped our midnight meetings.

12

The Just-in-Case Gun

By the end of that summer of death and clouded minds and cheap desire, I was desperate to leave Gibsland. But back at school, the fraternity that had commanded my loyalty was being undone. The girl I loved had left me. The political career I had envisioned seemed out of reach. All I had left was my new job as a journalist. I had done well as an intern, so the *Shreveport Times* offered me a part-time job — a full eight-hour shift three days a week — and I poured all my energy into it.

My shift started at one p.m. on Monday, Wednesday, and Friday, so I arranged to have my last classes end at noon on those days. That gave me sixty minutes to drive the sixty miles from school to work, west on I-20, passing Gibsland on the way. When my shift was over I'd often stop by my mother's house to get a plate of home cooking before continuing my drive back to school, to do homework into the middle of the night. This schedule kept me busy, and busy was what I needed.

Then, one day at the paper, the business editor dropped by my desk. He was a small black man who laughed more than other men, had buckteeth — the kind children get from sucking their thumb past the time they should outgrow it — and spoke with a lisp. He told me that the *New York Times* was sponsoring a job fair in Atlanta that weekend and that I "had to go." I told him that I couldn't, but he wouldn't take no for an answer.

I knew that the girlfriend of one of my line brothers had graduated and moved to Atlanta, so I made a deal: I would drive my line brother to Atlanta to visit her if they would let me sleep on her sofa when I got back from the job fair.

On the ride to Atlanta, we laughed and joked and talked in that deeper-than-normal way that the confines of a car make possible. A little over halfway there, somewhere in Alabama, we stopped for gas. My friend pumped it while I went to the bathroom. Among the graffiti on the wall was a sentence that jumped out at me: "Black pussy is good, but it smell funny."

There was something about it, the way the sentence was scrawled in barely legible penmanship, the way the *s* was missing from the word "smells." This was not a smart boy, I thought, not the kind Mrs. Collins would have smiled at. I had no idea who had written this, but I assumed that he wasn't black. He had presumed to objectify and ridicule a whole race of women, like those who had raised and loved me.

It was a strangely severe reaction for me to have to the scribbling, given how pervasive female objectification was in my world. The only difference here was that it overlapped with race. Race had not seemed a factor when the old men beneath the shade trees mumbled under their breath about girls they suspected of sleeping with "everything walking and half of what's standing still," or when the vile boys down the street crowded around the Sparrow girl's bed, not giving her time to "thank." Misogyny just seemed to hang on men like the rancid smell of rotting meat.

Still, there was something about this, about the racial part, that made it feel different. Not more or less wrong, but different. And it evoked my worst assumptions about that place: that it was one of the places between places, not a part of the world where racial hatchets had been buried and racial truces drawn, not a place like Gibs-land where blacks and whites had an understanding, not a place like Kiblah where Big Mama's and the Beales' respectful behavior disguised their financial arrangements. I imagined that this was one of the places where black women could still be simultaneously desired and despised, where lusts and fears produced dangerous interactions, where harsh stares tracked brown-bodied men from the slits of squinted eyes, where trees had not so long before been morbidly adorned with "strange fruit." I imagined that this was the kind of place the white boy who had yelled "Nigger!" and salted the ground between us must have been coming from or going to. This was Alabama, the state folks told me my great-grandfather had fled, running from the white tops one dark night, following a river and leaving his family.

The graffiti snapped the laughter out of me, and I drew up my shoulders. It made me realize that although the South was home, it was also hostile. I needed to get away, for a while at least, to see what my world looked like from the outside. It made me realize what the stakes really were for the job fair I was going to.

In Atlanta, my friend dropped me off at the job fair. At the door, a man told me that I couldn't enter because I hadn't applied beforehand, a process that included writing a sample essay and paying a fee. I asked for an application, found a corner, filled it out, wrote an essay, and gave the man the fee. He let me through.

I started on one side of the room, going to every booth for an interview. I explained to each of the newspaper recruiters my vision of combining traditional reporting with visual explanation, and got more than polite interest at almost every booth.

The New York Times representatives, however, had bad news for me. They said that I needed to have preregistered to be interviewed by them, and that all of their slots were filled. I politely said, "Oh, I understand. But, if you don't mind, I'm going to sit right here until someone doesn't show up." I took a seat to the side, picked up one of the free newspapers they were giving away, and began to read it.

I was well aware that my little stunt had caught the *Times* people off guard, and that they were watching me out of the corner of their eye. So I was careful to mind my manners and my posture, sitting up tall, managing a smile and a nod at the other students as they came and went. I sat there for nearly six hours. At the end of the day, the *Times* staff began to pack up. I still had the newspaper open in front of me, by then having read the same articles over and over.

One of the women relented: "Okay, okay, we'll interview you." "Oh, thank you," I said. I had watched dozens of other students be interviewed and overheard what the recruiters said when they left — what had impressed them and what had not — self-effacing cleverness and institutional reverence engaged them; boasting and deficient literary curiosity turned them off. It was invaluable opposition research that I wouldn't otherwise have gotten. Now that it was my turn, I showed them my work and told them about my then somewhat novel notion of combining visuals and journalism. When I was finished giving my pitch, the recruiter smiled a kind smile and told me that I was "very impressive" but that the *Times* just didn't have a graphics internship. I thanked her for her time and left for the evening. The fact that the *New York Times* thought a boy from Gibsland was "very impressive" was enough.

The next day, I went back to the job fair to visit some of the papers I'd missed because I had spent all my time sitting at the *Times*'s booth. But then I heard that the people from the *Times* were looking for me. So I went back to their booth. When I got there, the woman who'd interviewed me told me that although they didn't have a graphics internship, they were so impressed by me that they had called New York the night before and got the okay to create one.

I was going to New York in the summer to be the first graphics intern the *Times* had ever had.

I figured if I stayed busy for the rest of school and in my job in Shreveport, I could keep the depression — as I now knew to call it — at bay, and it worked. This would be a frame for much of the rest of my life: hard, focused, obsessive work to distract from a muddled private life. But still I had to go home and I had to sleep, and it was in that quiet time that the depression crept in on the backs of the male apparitions.

It was on one of those nights that the call came — Chester on the other end of the line, at my mother's house, him saying, "What's going on, boy?" like nothing had ever happened. That was the night the ball of pain in the pit of my stomach exploded in an uncontrollable conflagration, coming out not just in thoughts or words but with the ache of emotion and a flood of tears. That was the night I jumped in the car, grabbed the gun from under the car seat where I had kept it since my mother gave it to me because I refused to allow it in my house, and raced down Interstate 20 to kill Chester.

I had fired a gun only once before, on the Thanksgiving that Grandpa Bill took us deep into the woods to try his new pistol, the same day my mother and I raced down this same road, Interstate 20, trying to catch a woman who had slyly called on the phone and driven slowly by our house.

I thought then that I would never be able to shoot at a person, but now I knew that it was not only possible, but inevitable. This killing would be justifiable, in spirit if not in law.

I was about to kill Chester.

As I sped down the interstate toward my mother's house, the heat of my anguish being released into the winter air, I reviewed my simple plan — I would calmly walk into the house, find Chester, and shoot him in the head as many times as possible. No arguing. No explanations. Done.

By the time I reached the Grambling exit, I was bawling. I thought about all the emotional energy I had spent bracing myself against Chester's full-throated assaults and offhand insults. About all the times I had blamed myself for his betrayal. About who I was now, and who I could be. Seeing him lying in a pool of his own blood might finally liberate me from my past, but it would also destroy my future.

I had to make a choice: drive forward on the broad road toward the unspeakable or take the narrow highway exit. I don't know which chose, my head or my hand, but I exited and drove through the campus, thinking about all that I had accomplished. Me. With my own mind and grit. I had reinvented and improved myself. I was a man — a man with a future. I couldn't continue to live my life through the eyes of a seven-year-old boy.

I returned to my apartment and called a friend — not one of the Brothers but a girl from rural Arkansas whom I had befriended the semester before. We all called her Weezy because she looked so much like Isabel Sanford, who played Louise on *The Jeffersons*. She was big and brassy, sweet as pie but tough as nails. If I had a sister, I was sure that she would have acted like Weezy.

"Talk, Weezy. I don't care what you say. Just talk," I said.

She didn't ask questions. She just talked, as was her wont, for hours. I called her for that reason, and because I knew I wouldn't have to explain. The Brothers would have asked questions. That night, her ramblings helped save the life of a man she didn't even know.

That night, after I got off the phone with Weezy, I forced myself to come to terms with some things. Chester had done damage, but I wasn't dead, just different. Not worse, just different. He didn't deserve to die for what he had done, and I deserved to live in spite of it.

I had to learn to control my flashes of rage, to understand that gunshots created more problems than they solved, to decide that the ways of people on the west side of Gibsland were not necessarily the best ways. In the world beyond the train tracks and sweet potato farms, there were real rules and consequences. Self-righteousness wasn't license to do a wrong thing. The just-in-case moments in life didn't call for a gun, but guts.

I had to stop hating Chester to start loving myself. Forgiveness was freedom. Like my mother had done that Thanksgiving Day on the same interstate, I simply had to let go of my past so that I could step into my future.

Yes, the mark that Chester's betrayal had left on my life was likely permanent, but blaming him for the whole of the difference in my peculiar sexual identity, while convenient, was most likely not completely accurate. Abusers don't necessarily make children different in that way, but rather, they are diabolically gifted at detecting that kind of difference, often before the child can see it in him or herself, articulate it, and accept it. It is possible that Chester glimpsed a light in me, and that moved the darkness in him.

The male figures that sometimes came in the night were just a manifestation of a life lived in repression and pain and sadness, a part of me that lived in the shadows and on the fringes, because that's where I had confined it. But I had to let that part of me step out of the darkness, where I could see that it wasn't nearly as significant or as frightening as I had thought it was.

In addition to being attracted to women, I could also be attracted to men. There it was, all of it. That possibility of male attraction was such a simple little harmless idea, the fight against which I had allowed to consume and almost ruin my life. The attraction and my futile attempts to "fix it" had cost me my dreams. The anguish, combined with a lifetime of watching hotheads brandishing cold steel, had put me within minutes of killing a man.

My world had told me that there was nothing worse than not being all of one way, that any other way was the same as being dead, but my world had lied. I was very much alive. There was no hierarchy of humanity. There was no one way to be, or even two, but many. And no one could strip me of my value and dignity, because no one had bestowed them — these things came into the world with me.

I had done what the world had signaled I must — hidden the thorn in my flesh, held "the demon" at bay, kept the covenant, borne the weight of my crooked cross. But concealment makes the soul a swamp. Confession is how you drain it.

Daring to step into oneself is the bravest, strangest, most natural, most terrifying thing a person can do, because when you cease to wrap yourself in artifice you are naked, and when you are naked you are vulnerable.

But vulnerability is the leading edge of truth. Being willing to sacrifice a false life is the only way to live a true one.

I had to stop romanticizing the man I might have been and be the man that I was, not by neatly fitting other people's definitions of masculinity or constructs of sexuality, but by being uniquely me — made in the image of God, nurtured by the bosom of nature, and forged in the fire of life. I needed no cure because I had no infirmity. God need send no angel to trouble the water.

I had to summon the power that I believed Jed possessed — the power that was greater than all others. I had to stop running like the river, always wanting to be somewhere other than where I was, and just be the ocean — vast, deep, and exactly where it was always meant to be.

I had to start trying to live the Serenity Prayer, which Big Mama had hung by the door after Jed had coughed up the blood and gave up the ghost, the one about courage and change and acceptance.

I had to understand that there was no way to be a whole man without being an honest man. And I didn't have to wait to be proud to be honest. In fact, pride was not my aspiration. It was honor that I was after, the kind I had lost during the fraternity episodes when I had refused to stand up for what I felt was right because I was afraid that others would look at me like something was wrong. Never again.

I had to find the courage, too, to be me in the whole, refusing to conform or compromise, resisting the push and pull of the world around me. I had to assume the centrality of my singular position in it, the position that made me who I was, regardless of community or politics, acceptance or rejection.

I had spent my whole life trying to fit in, but it would take the rest of my life to realize that some men are just meant to stand out.

Whatever had shaped my identity, it was now all me. Trying to deny or control that fact was self-destructive. I would have to learn to simply relax and be: complex, betwixt and between, and absolutely all right.

I would have to learn to accept myself joyfully, fully, as the amalgamation of both the gifts and the tragedies of fate, as the person destiny had chosen me to be — gloriously rendered, deeply scarred, magnificently made, naturally flawed — a human being, my own man.

I would slowly learn to allow myself to follow attraction and curiosity wherever they might lead. I would grant myself latitude to explore the whole of me so that I could find the edges of me.

That would include attempts at male intimacy.

The first time I tried ended disastrously. I had worked up the nerve to go to a gay bar, thinking that if male intimacy was something my body wanted, I might as well know it.

It was a world apart from the one I knew. Instead of feeling a sense of belonging, I felt apart. The bar was brimming with sameness — not the locker room, frat house kind I was familiar with, full of ego-measuring and distance-keeping, but a different kind, which to me was disorienting. And the rules of engagement were at odds with what I was accustomed to: men sending signals in probing stares and touching before they spoke.

I was the object of considerable attention. I was young and tall and fit and new. I was being watched. I knew it, and I liked it. So I sat alone at the end of the bar and took long sips of my drink as I soaked up pensive admiration.

Soon a man sidled up to me and began making small talk. He was unremarkable in appearance and seemed slightly older than me. He said he was a shoe importer. He sounded smart and seemed kind, and he smiled a lot. He made it clear that he was interested in me, and invited me to his apartment for more drinks. I said, "Why not." In my mind, the moment I had walked through the door of the bar, I had passed the point of no return.

When we arrived at his house, he poured a glass of wine, but I was too nervous to drink it. He talked more about his business and showed me shoe samples — ugly, rough-cut sandals that I couldn't imagine anyone with even a dash of style deigning to wear.

Then, without warning, the mood shifted. The man disrobed, walked toward his bedroom, and beckoned me to follow. But the sight of him naked caused whatever attraction I might have had to collapse. His body looked sculpted, the way a body looks after years of proper eating and unstinting exercise, but I wasn't drawn to it. My body went limp and cold.

I could in no way imagine us intertwined. Who was to be the plug and who the socket — *not me!* — and how was the spark to be made? I found the idea of it all immensely unsettling. I was surprised by my reaction — embarrassed by it — but my feeling was unambiguous: I wasn't interested.

Instead of following him to the bedroom, I excused myself to go to the bathroom. Inside, I paced back and forth in a panic, realizing that I had gotten myself in deeper than my desires. I tried to think of a way to excuse myself from the situation with the least amount of fuss and hurt feelings, but I could think of none. Soon I burst out of the bathroom, yelled an excuse at the open bedroom door, grabbed my jacket, and ran out of the apartment.

I figured then that if I could indeed go both ways, one way didn't quite prefer to go all the way.

I would come to know what the world called people like me: bisexuals. The hated ones. The bastard breed. The "tragic mulattos" of sexual identity. Dishonest and dishonorable. Scandal-prone and disease-ridden. Nothing nice.

And while the word "bisexual" was technically correct, I would only slowly come to use it to refer to myself, in part because of the derisive connotations. But, in addition, it would seem to me woefully inadequate and impressionistically inaccurate. It reduced a range of identities, unbelievably wide and splendidly varied, in which same-gender attraction presented in graduated measures — from a pinch to a pound — to a single expression. To me it seemed too narrowly drawn in the collective consciousness, suggesting an identity fixed precisely in the middle between straight and gay, giving equal weight to each, bearing no resemblance to what I felt. In me, the attraction to men would never be equal to the attraction to women — in men it was often closer to the pinch — but it would always be in flux. Whenever someone got up the gumption to ask me outright, "What are you?" I'd reply with something coy: "Complicated." It would take many years before the word "bisexual" would roll off my tongue and not get stuck in my throat. I would have to learn that the designation wasn't only about sexual histories or current practice, but capacity. Nonetheless, when saying the word, I'd follow quickly with details meant to clarify.

Few people would be open to the idea of men like me even existing, in any incarnation. To many, I would be something like the Bigfoot from Boggy Creek — a loathsome thing some believed was real but most did not. Even the otherwise egalitarian would have no qualms about raising questions and casting doubt. Many could only conceive of bisexuality in the way it existed for most people willing to admit to it: as a transitory identity — a pit stop or a hiding place — and not a permanent one.

Whatever the case, folks would never truly understand me, nor I them.

To me, their limits on attraction would seem overly broad and arbitrary. To them, I would be a man who walked up to the water's edge and put only one foot in, out of fear or confusion or indecision. I would be the kind of man who wanted it all — clinging to the normative while nodding to difference.

But that's not the way it works within me. I wasn't moving, the same-gender attraction was. Sometimes it withdrew from me almost completely, and at others it lapped up to my knees. I wasn't making a choice; I was subject to the tide.

I wouldn't always get things right — I wouldn't always find the courage to tell people the whole truth about myself, or do so before their love had already reached through my secret and touched my shame — but at least I learned to move in the right direction. I wouldn't lay the weight of my shame down all at once, but a bit at a time over many years, like forks of hay pitched from the back of a pickup truck, until the bales dwindled and the load was made light.

I would get married fresh out of college — to Greta, the champagne-colored girl, the greatest love of my young life — after we both stopped pretending there was any other we would rather be with. I confessed to her my past and my proclivities, as fully as I understood them at the time, including the story of my encounter with the shoe importer, though not as soon as either of us would have preferred. We figured that our love was greater than my complexity. We had three beautiful children — an older boy and girl-boy twins — in rapid succession, but the marriage didn't survive the seventh year. We grew apart. Still, the marriage confirmed for me that extended fidelity was in fact possible, not by focusing on denying part of my nature but on submitting the whole of my heart. Monogamy was a choice. That was a side I could pick.

After Greta and I split, I decided to give male intimacy another try. The male attraction was still there, running alongside the female one — not equal, but there. I assumed my first failure might have been the result of youth and nerves and a mixed match. But now, again, my body sometimes failed to respond. Other times I was able to engage more fully, but almost always with the aid of copious amounts of alcohol, me barely able to remember the encounters and often wanting to forget them. This felt fraudulent to me, and opportunistic, and it was dangerous.

Still, no matter how much I drank, no matter how altered my consciousness, I couldn't completely rid myself of the unease of being intimately close to another man's body, hard and hairy and muscular and broad by the shoulders, more stem than flower — too much like my own.

In those moments I was acutely aware that I missed the primal tug of the female form, the primary sensation and the peripheral ones. The look of soft features and the feel of soft skin. The graceful slopes of supple curves. The sweet smells. The giggles. The thing in me that yearned for those sensory cues from a woman wouldn't quietly accept a substitute.

I once even found myself trying to imagine that a man who was interested in me was in fact a woman, so that I could get over my unease. That, to me, was going too far.

I had to accept a counterintuitive fact: my female attraction was fully formed — I could make love and fall in love — but my male attraction had no such terminus. I didn't think of men as romantic interests, and I would come to see my inhibitors around same-sex intercourse — whether congenitally imprinted or culturally constructed or some combination of those forces — as so high that I would quickly tire of trying to overcome them. To the degree that I held male attraction, it was frustrated. In that arena, I possessed no desire to submit and little to conquer. For years I worried that the barrier was some version of self-loathing, a denial. But eventually I concluded that the continual questioning — and attempts to circumvent it — was its own form of loathing, or self-flagellation. I would hold myself open to evolution on this point, but I would stop trying to force it. I would settle, over time, into the acceptance that my attractions, though fluid, were simply lopsided. Only with that acceptance would I truly feel free.

Furthermore, I'd come to understand that I sometimes confused the need for attention with a desire for sex. For much of my life I would crave attention with a carnal intensity. From anyone. From everyone. That feeling of being chosen. I would flirt with anyone who was congenial and amenable — a ravenous, indiscriminate flirtation, or a feather-light, barely-there one — or allow myself to be flirted with, by women and men alike, to cover the emptiness I felt or to fill in the hole, the desired culmination being not so much physical intimacy as emotional affirmation. The boy who had once felt invisible would forever ache simply to be seen.

But that would all come later. That school year, in the winter after Chester called and I raced down the highway with a gun before laying my burdens down, after the holidays were over and just as 1991 began, I left the just-in-case pistol in Gibsland, never to handle a gun again, and packed the car with clothes, some books, and a radio. My mother, the only woman I was sure truly loved me, waved goodbye, and I struck out for an internship at the *Wilmington News Journal* in Delaware, which was quickly followed by the summer internship at the *New York Times*.

I was finally headed up north, away from the places between places. As I snaked around the railroad track crossing arms, which were malfunctioning again that morning, I realized that I — the poor boy from the middle of nowhere, thrice betrayed — had made it, survived, rescued myself by dint of determination and the settling of my spirit.

After graduating, I took a job as a graphic artist at the *Detroit News,* where I practiced my own brand of visual journalism: combining reporting and writing with charts and diagrams. I would stay there one and a half winters — that was the way I counted it, because Detroit winters were the coldest this Louisiana boy had ever seen — before the *New York Times* hired me as a graphics editor. And, a few weeks before my twenty-fifth birthday, the *Times* put me in charge of the graphics department, making me the youngest newsroom department head the paper had ever had. I would leave the *Times* briefly for a stint as art director of *National Geographic* magazine before returning to the *Times* for a novel role created for me, producing charts and offering my written opinion about what they meant and why it mattered — a "visual op-ed columnist," they called me. By a twist of fate, I found my way back to writing.

At Grambling, my fraternity was suspended after more hazing a few years after I left. The suspension would last until all the current members had graduated and the chapter could start anew. Chopper went on to become a prominent corporate lawyer, Clay became a successful banker and the godfather of my oldest son, and Kaboom a television producer and the godfather of my daughter.

In Gibsland, my mother became a pillar of the community even as the small town contracted around her. She continued her learning and teaching. In retirement she volunteered as a teachers' aide and substitute teacher before running for a spot on the local school board, and winning.

Gibsland as I remember it has almost vanished, leaving not much more than another wide place in the road. All but one of the one-of-each-thing stores have shuttered their doors. The sweet potato farms have ceased production, and the upholstery shop is gone. The House with No Steps has been torn down, and my mother purposely burned Papa Joe's house to the ground rather than maintain it.

White folks in town slowly moved away or died off, and black folks began to buy the vacated houses, a kind of integration by attrition, but the chain link fence separating the white and black cemeteries remains.

My four brothers stayed in the South, all within driving distance of my mother, and they have all become devoted fathers, like I have tried to be, although only Nathan, James, and I ever married, and only Nathan's marriage survived.

Big Mama and Grandpa Joe have died. Aunt Odessa and Mrs. Bertha and Sun Buddy and all the old people with whom I spent my days are gone. Uncle Paul also has died. Folks have told me that Evelyn married a man named Loved a few months after leaving Gibsland with her baby. I never saw or heard from Chester again.

My parents have moved gently into old age. My mother has become the kind of grandmother who is quick to let her feelings show, saying "I miss you," "I'm proud of you," and "I love you" unguardedly. My father has become a doting grandfather — one who gives hugs and rides on his knees and who takes the grandchildren to the store to buy more candy than we parents allow. And he's become a Bible-toting deacon at the church where I was baptized.

My parents have reconciled to some degree. They were never again romantically involved, but they developed a loving relationship. My father still brought food, even after my brothers and I were gone from home. My mother makes him plates whenever she has extra. She chastises him for being a scoundrel when they were younger. He takes it without retorting or retreating — his way of showing remorse. He has stopped squandering money, and occasionally shares a little. She does his taxes. A relationship that was afflicted in youth has become cured by age.

As their kindness to each other grew in the shadow of bad memories, they demonstrated the resilience of love, the power of forgiveness, and the possibility of moving forward and growing in grace.

When I called my mother to tell her about this book, as I was finishing it, and to tell her about Chester's and Uncle Paul's betrayals, and the way that I had come to consider myself, she asked rhetorically, her voice quivering and full of ache: "And you didn't think you could tell me?"

She cried.

A couple of weeks later, my father called me for the first time in my adult life. I was sure that my mother had told him about our conversation, because I knew they now discussed things with civility and concern. But he didn't let on. When I answered the phone, he said, "Char'es. It's me. You jus' run across my mind, so I needed to call and check on my boy."

I cried.

· · ·

As my parents transcended who they'd been, they provided a path for me to do the same. My role as a columnist quickly evolved, so that my prose held more weight than the accompanying visuals. I would write mostly about politics, because I had long been fascinated by it, but I would also allow the column to be a digest of my interests and experiences, sometimes extremely personal ones, all of me. I would highlight the plight of children like the one I had been — the poor, the lost, the most vulnerable. I would advocate for the equal and honorable treatment of those who thought themselves different, because I thought myself different. I would warn against the dangers of gun-saturated societies, because I had grown up in and operated in one. I would caution about the corrosive effects of hazing, because I'd participated in it. I would exalt teachers, because one had reached out and saved me. I would campaign against bullying, because it had nearly destroyed me. And I would write about parenting, because being a father gave my life profound purpose and centered me.

I would harness the truths that had been trapped in me like a fire shut up in my bones. I would give my life over to my passions, my writing, and my children, and they would breathe life back into me.